Pedigree

English translations of works by Patrick Modiano

From Yale University Press
After the Circus
Paris Nocturne
Pedigree
Suspended Sentences

Also available or forthcoming
The Black Notebook
Catherine Certitude
Dora Bruder
Honeymoon
In the Café of Lost Youth
Lacombe Lucien
Missing Person
Out of the Dark
So You Don't Get Lost in the Neighborhood
The Occupation Trilogy (The Night Watch,
    Ring Roads, and La Place de l'Etoile)
Villa Triste
Young Once

Pedigree
A Memoir

Patrick Modiano

*Translated from the French
by Mark Polizzotti*

Yale UNIVERSITY PRESS · NEW HAVEN AND LONDON

A MARGELLOS
WORLD REPUBLIC OF LETTERS BOOK

The Margellos World Republic of Letters is dedicated to making
literary works from around the globe available in English through
translation. It brings to the English-speaking world the work of
leading poets, novelists, essayists, philosophers, and playwrights
from Europe, Latin America, Africa, Asia, and the Middle East
to stimulate international discourse and creative exchange.

Yale University Press books may be purchased in quantity for educational,
business, or promotional use. For information, please e-mail sales.press@
yale.edu (U.S. office) or sales@yaleup.co.uk (U.K. office).

Set in MT Baskerville type by Tseng Information Systems, Inc.
Printed in the United States of America.

Library of Congress Control Number: 2015934999
ISBN 978-0-300-21533-5 (cloth : alk. paper)

A catalogue record for this book is available from the British Library. This
paper meets the requirements of ANSI/NISO Z39.48-1992 (Permanence of
Paper).

10 9 8 7 6 5 4 3 2 1

Pedigree

I was born on July 30, 1945, at 11 Allée Marguerite in Boulogne-Billancourt, to a Jewish man and a Flemish woman who had met in Paris under the Occupation. I write "Jewish" without really knowing what the word meant to my father, and because at the time it was what appeared on the identity papers. Periods of great turbulence often lead to rash encounters, with the result that I've never felt like a legitimate son, much less an heir.

My mother was born in 1918 in Antwerp. She spent her childhood in a suburb of that city, between Kiel and Hoboken. Her father was a laborer, then assistant surveyor. Her maternal grandfather, Louis Bogaerts, was a dockworker; he posed for the statue of the longshoreman by Constantin Meunier that stands in front of the Antwerp city hall. I've kept his *loonboek* for the year 1913, in which he recorded the names of all the ships he unloaded: the *Michigan*, the *Elisabethville*, the *Santa Anna* . . . He died on the job, at around age sixty-five, from a fall.

As a teenager, my mother joined the Fau-
cons Rouges youth group. She worked for the
gas company. In the evenings, she took drama
classes. In 1938, she was signed by the film-
maker and producer Jan Vanderheyden to act
in his Flemish "comedies." Four films between
1938 and 1941. She was a chorus girl in music
hall revues in Antwerp and Brussels; there were
many German refugees among the dancers and
artists. In Antwerp, she shared a small house on
Horenstraat with two friends: a dancer, Joppie
Van Allen, and Leon Lemmens, who was more
or less the secretary and shill of a rich homo-
sexual, the baron Jean L., and who would be
killed in a bombardment in Ostend in May 1940.
Her best friend was a young decorator, Lon Lan-
dau, whom she'd meet again in Brussels in 1942
wearing the yellow star.

I'm trying to follow chronological order, for
want of other reference points. In 1940, once
Belgium was occupied, she lived in Brussels.
She became engaged to a certain Georges Niels,
who at age twenty managed a hotel, the Canter-

bury. The hotel restaurant was partly commandeered by officers of the Propaganda-Staffel. My mother lived in the Canterbury and met various people there. I know nothing about all those people. She worked in radio, playing in Flemish broadcasts. She was hired by a theater in Ghent. In June 1941, she was in a theatrical tour of the ports along the Atlantic and the English Channel, performing for Flemish workers of the Organisation Todt and, farther north, in Hazebrouck, for German airmen.

She was a pretty girl with an arid heart. Her fiancé had given her a chow-chow, but she didn't take care of it and left it with various people, as she would later do with me. The chow-chow killed itself by leaping from a window. The dog appears in two or three photos, and I have to admit that he touches me deeply and that I feel a great kinship with him.

Georges Niel's parents, rich hotel owners from Brussels, did not want their son to marry her. She decided to leave Belgium. The Germans intended to send her to film school in Ber-

lin, but a young officer from the Propaganda-
Staffel whom she'd met in the Canterbury got
her out of that predicament by sending her to
Paris, to Continental Films, a production company, run by Alfred Greven.

She arrived in Paris in June 1942. Greven
gave her a screen test at the Billancourt studios,
but it wasn't very convincing. She worked in the
"dubbing" department at Continental, writing
Dutch subtitles for the French films the company produced. She became the girlfriend of
Aurel Bischoff, one of Greven's assistants.

In Paris, she lived in a room at 15 Quai de
Conti, in an apartment rented by an antiques
dealer from Brussels and his friend Jean de B.,
whom I can picture as a teenager, with a mother
and sisters in a chateau in the heart of Poitou,
writing fervent letters to Jean Cocteau in secret.
Through Jean de B., my mother met a young
German, Klaus Valentiner, who had secured a
cushy administrative post. He lived in a studio
on the Quai Voltaire and, in his leisure time,

read the latest novels by Evelyn Waugh. He was later sent to the Russian Front and was killed.

Other visitors to the Quai de Conti apartment included a young Russian, Georges d'Ismailoff, who was tubercular but always went out into the frozen winters of the Occupation without an overcoat. A Greek, Christos Bellos: he had missed the last ship leaving for America, where he was supposed to join a friend. A girl of the same age, Geneviève Vaudoyer. All that remains of them are their names. Geneviève Vaudoyer and her father, Jean-Louis Vaudoyer, were the first French bourgeois family to invite my mother to their home. Geneviève Vaudoyer introduced my mother to Arletty, who also lived on the Quai de Conti, in the building next door to number 15. Arletty took my mother under her wing.

I hope I can be forgiven all these names, and others to follow. I'm a dog who pretends to have a pedigree. My mother and father didn't belong to any particular milieu. So aimless were

they, so unsettled, that I'm straining to find a
few markers, a few beacons in this quicksand, as
one might attempt to fill in with half-smudged
letters a census form or administrative question-
naire.

My father was born in 1912, in Square Pé-
trelle in Paris, on the border of the 9th and 10th
arrondissements. His father was originally from
Thessaloniki and belonged to a Jewish family
from Tuscany established under the Ottoman
Empire. Cousins in London, Alexandria, Milan,
Budapest. Four of my father's cousins, Carlo,
Grazia, Giacomo, and his wife, Mary, would
be murdered by the SS in Italy, in Arona, on
Lake Maggiore, in September 1943. My grandfather left Thessaloniki when he was a child and
went to Alexandria. But after several years, he
left for Venezuela. I believe he had cut all ties
with his family and background. He became in-
volved in the pearl trade in Margarita Island,
then ran a thrift shop in Caracas. After Venezuela, he settled in Paris in 1903. He ran an antiques shop at 5 Rue de Châteaudun, where he

sold objets d'art from China and Japan. He held a Spanish passport, and until the day he died he would be registered at the Spanish consulate in Paris, whereas his forebears, as "Tuscan subjects," had been under the protection of the French, English, and then Austrian consulates. I've kept several of his passports, one of which was issued by the Spanish consulate in Alexandria. And a certificate, drawn up in Caracas in 1894, attesting that he was a member of the Society for the Prevention of Cruelty to Animals. My grandmother was born in the Pas-de-Calais. In 1916, her father lived in a suburb of Nottingham. But after her marriage, she adopted Spanish citizenship.

My father lost his father when he was four. Childhood in the 10th arrondissement, Cité d'Hauteville. Collège Chaptal, where he was a boarder—even on weekends, he told me. And from his dormitory he could hear the music of the street carnival, on the median strip along Boulevard des Batignolles. He never took his baccalaureate exam. As a teenager and young

adult, he was left to his own devices. By age six-
teen, he and his friends were hanging out at the
Hôtel Bohy-Lafayette, the bars of Faubourg
Montmartre, the Cadet, the Luna Park. His
name was Alberto, but they called him Aldo. At
age eighteen, he began smuggling petroleum,
sneaking drums of it into Paris undetected by the
authorities. At nineteen, he asked a manager of
the Saint-Phalle bank to underwrite his "financial" operations, so persuasively that the latter
agreed to back him. But the affair went sour,
as my father was a minor, and the law stepped
in. At age twenty-four, he rented a room at 33
Avenue Montaigne and, according to certain
documents I've preserved, he often traveled to
London to help form a company called Bravisco
Ltd. His mother died in 1937 in a boardinghouse
on Rue Roquépine, where he had lived for a
time with his brother Ralph. Then he had taken
a room in the Hôtel Terminus, near the Gare
Saint-Lazare, which he'd left without settling his
bill. Just before the war, he took over manage-
ment of a shop selling stockings and perfume at

71 Boulevard Malesherbes. It seems he was then residing on Rue Frédéric-Bastiat, in the 8th.

And war broke out at a time when he had no capital whatsoever and was already living by his wits. In 1940, he had his mail sent to the Hôtel Victor-Emmanuel III at 24 Rue de Ponthieu. In a letter of that year to his brother Ralph, sent from Angoulême where he was stationed in an artillery regiment, he mentioned a chandelier that they'd pawned. In another letter, he asked to have the *Courier des pétroles* forwarded to him in Angoulême. In 1937–39, he was in "business" with a certain Enriquez, the Société Royalieu, dealing in Romanian petroleum.

The fall of France in June 1940 caught him in his barracks in Angoulême. He was not taken away in the mass of prisoners, as the Germans didn't arrive in Angoulême until after the armistice was signed. He took refuge in Les Sables-d'Olonne, where he stayed until September. There he ran into his friend Henri Lagroua and two girls they knew, one called Suzanne and the other Gysèle Hollerich, a dancer at the Tabarin.

Back in Paris, he did not register with the authorities as a Jew. He lived with his brother Ralph, at the home of Ralph's girlfriend, a Mauritian with a British passport. The apartment was at 5 Rue des Saussaies, right next to the Gestapo. Because of her British passport, the Mauritian had to appear at police headquarters every week; she would be detained for several months in Besançon and Vittel as an "Englishwoman." My father had a girlfriend, Hela H., a German Jew who had been engaged to Billy Wilder back in Berlin. They were picked up during a raid one evening in February 1942, in a restaurant on Rue de Marignan, during an identity check — which were frequent that month because of the new regulations forbidding Jews from being out on the street or in public after 8 P.M. My father and his girlfriend were not carrying any papers. They were carted off in a Black Maria by police inspectors, who brought them to Rue Greffulhe for "verification," before a certain Superintendent Schweblin. My father had to state his identity. He got separated from his girlfriend and managed to escape as they were about to transfer him to the "Depot," the holding tank, taking advantage of a moment when the hall light went out. Hela H. would be released from the Depot the next day, probably on a word from a friend of her father's. Who? I've often wondered. After his escape, my father hid under the staircase of a building on Rue des Mathurins, trying not to attract the notice of the concierge. He spent the night there because of the curfew. In the morning, he went home to 5 Rue des Saussaies. Then he hid out with the Mauritian and his brother Ralph in a hotel, the Alcyon de Breteuil, whose manageress was the mother of a friend of theirs. Later, he lived with Hela H. in a furnished room on Square Villaret-de-Joyeuse and at the Marronniers on Rue de Chazelles.

Among the people he knew at the time, the ones I've managed to identify are Henri Lagroua; Sacha Gordine; Freddie McEvoy, an Australian bobsled champion and racing driver with whom he shared an "office" on the Champs-Elysées right after the war (I've never been able to determine the name of the company); a certain Jean Koporindé, 189 Rue de la Pompe; Geza Pellmont; Toddie Werner (who called herself "Mme Sahuque") and her friend Hessien (Liselotte); and a Russian girl, Kissa Kuprin, daughter of the writer Aleksandr Kuprin. She had acted in a few films and in one of Roger Vitrac's plays, *Les Demoiselles du large.* Flory Francken, aka Nardus, whom my father called Flo, was the daughter of a Dutch painter. She had spent her childhood and adolescence in Tunisia, then had come to Paris and hung out in Montparnasse. In 1938, she'd been implicated in a minor incident that had landed her in criminal court, and in 1940 she had married the Japanese actor Sessue Hayakawa. During the Occupation, she was close to the actress Dita Parlo, who had starred in *L'Atalante,* and her lover Dr. Fuchs, one of the directors of the so-called Otto Bureau, the most important of the black market "purchasing services," located at 6 Rue Adolphe-Yvon in the 16th arrondissement.

This was more or less the world in which my

father circulated. Demimonde? Underworld? Before she is lost in the cold night of oblivion, I'll mention another Russian, who was his girlfriend at the time: Galina "Gay" Orloff. She had immigrated to the United States when very young. At twenty, she was dancing in a burlesque club in Florida, where she met a small, dark man, very sentimental and courteous, whose mistress she became: a certain Lucky Luciano. Back in Paris, she had worked as a model and married to obtain French citizenship. At the start of the Occupation, she lived with a Chilean "secretary of legation," Pedro Eyzaguirre, then on her own at the Hôtel Chateaubriand on Rue du Cirque, where my father often went to see her. A few months after I was born she gave me a teddy bear that I long held onto as a talisman and my only souvenir of an absent mother. She took her life on February 12, 1948, at age thirty-four. She is buried in Sainte-Geneviève-des-Bois.

The more I draw up this list of names and call the roll in an empty garrison, the more my head spins and my breath grows short. Curious individuals. Curious times, neither fish nor fowl. And my parents came to know each other during that period, among those people who were like them. Two lost, heedless butterflies in the midst of an indifferent city. *Die Stadt ohne Blick.* But there's nothing I can do about it: that's the soil—or the dung—from which I emerged. Most of the scraps of their lives that I've been able to gather, I get from my mother. But there was much she didn't know about the murky, clandestine world of the black market in which my father traveled by force of circumstance. She was unaware of most of it. And he took his secrets to the grave.

They met one evening in October 1942, at the home of Toddie Werner, aka Mme Sahuque, at 28 Rue Scheffer, 16th arrondissement. My father was carrying an identity card in the name of his friend Henri Lagroua. On the glass door of the concierge's lodge at 15 Quai de Conti, the name "Henri Lagroua" had been listed among the tenants since the Occupation, next to the words "fourth floor." When I was a child, I asked the concierge who this "Henri Lagroua" was. He answered, "Your father." This dual identity had impressed me at the time. Much later, I learned that during that period he'd used other names by which certain people still knew him well after the war. But names end up becoming detached from the poor mortals who bore them and they glimmer in our imaginations like distant stars. My mother introduced my father to Jean de B. and her friends. They thought there was something "weird and South American" about him and gently cautioned my mother to "be careful." She repeated this to my father, who joked that the next time he would "look even weirder" and "scare them even worse."

He was not South American, but having no legal existence, he lived off the black market. My mother would pick him up at one of the tiny offices reached via the multitude of elevators along the arcades of the Lido. He was always there with several others whose names I don't know. He was mainly in touch with a "purchasing service" at 53 Avenue Hoche, the office of two Armenian brothers he'd known before the war: Alexandre and Ivan S. Among the goods he delivered to them were entire truckloads of old ball bearings lifted from expired stock of the SKF company, which would sit uselessly in a warehouse in Saint-Ouen, gathering rust. In the course of my research, I came across the names of a few individuals who worked at 53 Avenue Hoche — Baron Wolff, Dante Vannuchi, Doctor Patt, "Alberto" — and wondered whether these weren't just more of my father's pseudonyms. It was in this purchasing service on Avenue Hoche that he met a certain André Gabison, the manager of the establishment, whom he often mentioned to my mother. I once got hold of a list of German Special Forces agents dating from 1945, which contained a note about this man: Gabison, André. Italian national, born 1907. Merchant. Passport no. 13755, issued in Paris on 11/18/42, listing him as a Tunisian businessman. Since 1940, associate of Richir (purchasing service, 53 Avenue Hoche). In 1942, in St. Sebastian as Richir's contact. In April 1944, worked under the command of a certain Rados of the SD; traveled frequently between Hendaye and Paris. In August 1944, reported as belonging to the sixth section of the Madrid SD under the command of Martin Maywald. Address: Calle Jorge Juan 17, Madrid (tel.: 50-222).

My father's other acquaintances under the Occupation, at least the ones I know about: an Italian banker, Georges Giorgini-Schiff, and his girlfriend, Simone, who would later marry Pierre Foucret, the owner of the Moulin Rouge. Giorgini-Schiff had his offices at 4 Rue de Penthièvre. My father bought a large pink diamond from him, the "Southern Cross," which he'd try to resell after the war, when he was destitute. Giorgini-Schiff was arrested by the Germans in September 1943, following the Italian armistice. During the Occupation, he had introduced my parents to a Doctor Carl Gerstner, economic adviser at the German embassy, whose girlfriend, Sybil, was Jewish, and who would apparently become a "major" figure in East Berlin after the war. Annet Badel: former attorney, director of the Théâtre du Vieux-Colombier in 1944. My father did some black marketeering with him and his son-in-law, Georges Vikar. Badel had sent my mother a typescript of Sartre's *No Exit*, which he planned to stage at the Vieux-Colombier in May 1944, under its initial title, "Other People." That script of "Other People" was still lying at the back of a wardrobe in my room on the fifth floor of Quai de Conti when I was fifteen. Badel thought my mother kept in touch with the Germans through the Continental Films production company, and that she could help him obtain a censorship visa for the play more quickly.

Other close associates of my father's: André Camoin, antiques dealer, Quai Voltaire; Maria Chernichev, a daughter of Russian nobility but "déclassée," with whom he conducted some huge black market deals; and a certain "M. Fouquet," with whom he conducted more modest ones. This Fouquet had a shop on Rue de Rennes and lived in a small private house in the Paris suburbs.

I close my eyes and I see Lucien P. arriving, with his heavy footstep, from the deepest recesses of the past. I believe his job consisted of acting as middleman and introducing people to one another. He was very fat, and in my childhood, whenever he sat on a chair I was always afraid it would collapse under his weight. When he and my father were young, Lucien P. was the long-suffering lover of the actress Simone Simon, whom he followed around like a big poodle. And also a friend of Sylviane Quimfe, a pool shark and adventuress, who under the Occupation would become the Marquise d'Abrantès and the mistress of one of the Rue Lauriston gang. People on whom you can't dwell at length. Shady travelers at best, passing through a train station concourse without my ever knowing their final destination, supposing they even had one. To finish with this list of phantoms, I should mention the two brothers, who might have been twins: Ivan and Alexandre S. The latter had a girlfriend, Inka, a Finnish dancer. They must have been real *grands seigneurs* of the black mar-

ket, because under the Occupation they cele-
brated their "first billion" in an apartment in the
massive edifice at 1 Avenue Paul-Doumer, where
Ivan S. lived. He fled to Spain at the Liberation,
as did André Gabison. As for Alexandre S., I
wonder what became of him. But is there really
any point asking? *My* heart goes out to those
whose faces appeared on the German wanted
posters, the "Affiche Rouge."

Jean de B. and the antiques dealer from Brussels left the apartment on the Quai de Conti in
early 1943, and my parents moved in. Before I
finally get sick of all this and no longer have the
heart or the energy to continue, here are a few
more scraps of their life at that distant time, but
as they lived it in the chaos of the present.

They sometimes hid out in Ablis, at the
Chateau du Bréau, with Henri Lagroua and
his girlfriend Denise. The Chateau du Bréau
was abandoned. It belonged to some Ameri-
cans who had fled France because of the war
and given them the keys. In the countryside,
my mother took motorcycle rides with La-

groua on his 500 cc BSA. She spent the months of July and August 1943 with my father at an inn in Varenne-Saint-Hilaire, the Petit Ritz. Giorgini-Schiff, Simone, Gerstner, and his girlfriend, Sybil, joined them there. Swimming in the Marne. The inn was home to several outlaws and their "wives," among whom a certain "Didi" and his companion, "Mme Didi." The men drove away in the morning to attend to their dirty work and returned from Paris very late at night. Once, my parents overheard an argument in the room above theirs. A woman called her man a "lousy cop" and threw wads of cash out the window, berating him for bringing back all that money. Police stooges? Gestapo henchmen? Toddie Werner, aka Mme Sahuque, at whose home my parents had met, barely managed to avoid being picked up at the beginning of 1943. She injured herself jumping from a window of her apartment. There was a warrant out for the arrest of one of my father's oldest friends, Sacha Gordine, as attested by a memo from the Legal Status Bureau in the General Commis-

sariat for Jewish Affairs to the head of an "Investigation and Verification Division": "April 6,
1944. Per the above-referenced note, I had re-
quested that you proceed without delay to arrest
the Jew Sacha Gordine for infraction of the Law
of June 2, 1941. Pursuant to this note, you in-
dicated that this individual had abandoned his
present domicile without leaving a forwarding
address. However, he has lately been observed
riding his bicycle in the streets of Paris. I therefore request that you kindly pay another visit to
his domicile so as to follow up on my note of
January 25th last."

I remember that my father mentioned this
period, once only, one evening when we were
on the Champs-Elysées. He pointed out the end
of Rue de Marignan, where they had taken him
away in February 1942. And he told me of a second arrest, in the winter of 1943, after "someone" had denounced him. He had been brought
to the Depot, from where "someone" had freed
him. That evening, I felt that he wanted to un-
burden himself, but the words wouldn't come.

He said only that the Black Maria had made the rounds of the police stations before reaching the lockup. At one of the stops, a young girl had got on and sat across from him. Much later I tried, in vain, to pick up her trace, not knowing whether it was the evening in 1942 or in 1943.

In the spring of 1944, my father received anonymous telephone calls at the Quai de Conti. A voice addressed him by his real name. One afternoon, when he was out, two French plainclothesmen rang at the door and asked for M. Modiano. My mother told them she was just a young Belgian working at Continental, a German company. She was subletting a room in the apartment from a man named Henri Lagroua and couldn't help them. They promised to come back. My father, to avoid them, left the Quai de Conti. I imagine these were not members of Schweblin's Jewish Affairs police but men from the Investigation and Verification Division—as in Sacha Gordine's case. Or else they were sent by Superintendent Permilleux of the Prefecture. Later, I tried to put faces to all those names, but they remained firmly ensconced in the shadows, with their odor of rotten leather.

My parents resolved to leave Paris as quickly as possible. Christos Bellos, the Greek my mother had met at B.'s, knew a girl who lived on a property near Chinon. The three of them took refuge with her. My mother brought along her winter sportswear, in case they had to flee even farther. They hid in that house in the Touraine until the Liberation and would return to Paris, on bicycles, only when the American troops arrived.

Back in Paris at the beginning of September 1944, my father was hesitant about returning right away to the Quai de Conti, fearing that the police would again be after him—this time because of his illegal activities as a black marketeer. My parents lived in a hotel at the corner of Avenue de Breteuil and Avenue Duquesne, the same Alcyon de Breteuil where my father had already hid out in 1942. He sent my mother on ahead to Quai de Conti to get the lay of the land. She was summoned by the police and subjected to a lengthy interrogation. Since she was a foreigner, they wanted to know the precise reason for her arrival in Paris in 1942 under German patronage. She explained that she was engaged to a Jew with whom she'd been living for two years. The police questioning her were no doubt colleagues of the ones who'd tried to arrest my father under his real name a few months earlier. Or the same ones. They must now have been searching for him through his aliases, unable to identify him.

They released my mother. That evening at the hotel, beneath their windows, women strolled with American GIs along the median strip running down Avenue de Breteuil, and one of them tried to make an American understand how many months they'd been waiting for them. She counts on her fingers in English: "*One, two* . . ." But the American doesn't get it and instead imitates her, counting on his own fingers: *One, two, three, four* . . . And so on and so forth. After several weeks, my father left the Alcyon de Breteuil. Back at the Quai de Conti, he dis-

covered that his Ford, which he'd stashed in a
garage in Neuilly, had been commandeered in
June by the Vichy militia, the Milice, and it was
in that Ford, its bullet-riddled body impounded
as evidence by the investigating detectives, that
Georges Mandel had been assassinated.

On August 2, 1945, my father went by bike to register my birth at the town hall of Boulogne-Billancourt. I imagine him returning through the deserted streets of Auteuil and alongside the silent quays of that summer.

Then he decided we'd live in Mexico. The passports were ready. At the last minute, he changed his mind. He came this close to leaving Europe after the war. Thirty years later, he went to die in Switzerland, a neutral country. In the meantime, he moved around a lot: Canada, Guyana, Equatorial Africa, Colombia . . . He was searching for El Dorado, in vain. And I wonder whether he wasn't also trying to flee the Occupation years. He never told me what he had felt, deep inside, in Paris during that period. Fear? The strange sensation of being hunted simply because someone had classified him as a specific type of prey, when he himself didn't really know what he was? But one shouldn't speak for others and I've always been reticent about breaking silences, even when they do you harm.

Nineteen forty-six. My parents were still living at 15 Quai de Conti, on the fourth and fifth floors. In 1947, my father would also rent the third floor. My father's relative and rather fleeting prosperity lasted until that year, at which point he entered what they call "splendid poverty." He worked with Giorgini-Schiff, with one M. Tessier, a citizen of Costa Rica, and with a baron Louis de la Rochette. He was the close friend of a certain Z., who was mixed up in the "wine scandal" of 1946. My maternal grandparents came to Paris from Antwerp to look after me. I spent all my time with them, and I spoke only Flemish. In 1947, on October 5, my brother, Rudy, was born. Since the Liberation, my mother had been taking acting classes at the Vieux-Colombier school. In 1946 she landed a minor role in *Auprès de ma blonde* at the Théâtre de la Michodière. In 1949, she had a bit part in the film *Rendezvous in July*.

That summer of 1949, in Cap-d'Antibes and on the Côte Basque, she spent time with a play-boy of Russian origin, Vladimir Rachevsky, and with the marquis d'A., a Basque who wrote poetry. That's something I would learn later on. We stayed alone in Biarritz for nearly two years, my brother and I. We lived in a small apartment in the Casa Montalvo, and the woman who looked after us was the caretaker of that house. I don't have a very clear memory of her face.

In September 1950, we were baptized at the church of Saint-Martin in Biarritz, without my parents being present. According to the baptism certificate, my godfather was a mysterious "Jean Minthe," whom I didn't know. In October 1950 I went to school for the first time, at Sainte-Marie de Biarritz, in the Casa Montalvo neighborhood.

One afternoon when school let out, there was no one waiting for me. I tried to go home on my own, but as I crossed the street I was knocked down by a van. The driver brought me back to the nuns, who placed an ether-soaked pad over my face to put me to sleep. Since then, I've been quite sensitive to the smell of ether. Overly sensitive. Ether has the curious ability to remind me of pain, then immediately erase it. Memory and amnesia.

We returned to Paris in 1951. One Sunday afternoon I was in the wings of the Théâtre Montparnasse, where my mother was playing a small part in *Le Complexe de Philémon*. My mother was onstage. I got scared and started to cry. Suzanne Flon, who was also in the cast, gave me a postcard to quiet me down.

The apartment on the Quai de Conti. On the third floor, in the evening, we heard voices and bursts of laughter from the room next to ours, where my mother entertained her friends from Saint-Germain-des-Prés. I seldom saw her. I can't recall a single act of genuine warmth or protectiveness from her. I was always on my guard around her. Her sudden flares of temper upset me deeply, and since I went to catechism, I prayed for God to forgive her. The fourth floor was where my father had his office. He was often there with two or three others. They sat in armchairs or on the arms of the sofa, talking among themselves. They took turns making phone calls. And they tossed the receiver back and forth to each other, like a rugby ball. Now and then, my father would hire young girls, students at the Beaux-Arts, to look after us. He had them answer the phone and say he "wasn't there." He dictated his letters to them.

At the start of 1952, my mother handed us over to a friend, Suzanne Bouquerau, who lived in a house at 38 Rue du Docteur-Kurzenne, in Jouy-en-Josas. I attended the Jeanne-d'Arc school at the end of the street, and after that the local public school. My brother and I were choirboys at midnight Mass in 1952, in the village church. First readings: *The Last of the Mohicans*, which I found incomprehensible but read all the way to the end. *The Jungle Book*. Andersen's fairy tales illustrated by Adrienne Ségur. Aymé's *The Wonderful Farm*.

Strange women came and went at 38 rue du Docteur-Kurzenne, among them Zina Rachevsky; Suzanne Baulé, known as Frede, the manager of Carroll's, a nightspot on Rue de Ponthieu; and a certain Rose-Marie Krawell, owner of a hotel on Rue du Vieux-Colombier, who drove an American car. They wore men's jackets and shoes, and Frede wore a tie. We played with Frede's nephew.

From time to time, my father would come visit us accompanied by his friends and a sweet young blonde, Nathalie, an airline stewardess he'd met on one of his trips to Brazzaville. On Thursday afternoons, we listened to children's programs on the radio. On other days, I sometimes heard the news broadcasts. The announcer was reporting the trial of those who had committed the MASSACRE AT ORADOUR. The sound of those words freezes my blood, today as much as it did back then, when I didn't really understand what they meant.

One evening, during one of his visits, my father was sitting across from me in the living room of the house on Rue du Docteur-Kurzenne, near the bow window. He asked what I wanted to do with my life. I didn't know what to answer.

One morning in February 1953, my father came to collect us, my brother and me, in the empty house, and drove us back to Paris. Later, I learned that Suzanne Bouquerau had been arrested for burglary. Between Jouy-en-Josas and Paris, the mystery of those suburbs that weren't yet suburbs. The ruined chateau and, in front of it, the tall grass in the meadow where we flew our kite. The woods at Les Metz. And the large wheel of the water mill in Marly, which spun with the noise and coolness of a waterfall.

From 1953 to 1956 we lived in Paris, and my brother and I attended the local school on Rue du Pont-de-Lodi. We also took catechism at the church of Saint-Germain-des-Prés. We often saw Father Pachaud, who officiated at Saint-Germain-des-Prés and lived in a studio on Rue Bonaparte. I found a letter that Father Pachaud wrote to me at the time. "Monday, July 18. I imagine you must be building sandcastles on the beach. . . . When the tide comes in, the best you can do is run for it! It's like when the whistle blows at the end of recess in the schoolyard of Pont-de-Lodi! Did you know it's very hot in Paris right now? Luckily we get storms from time to time that cool down the temperature. If Catechism were still ongoing, you'd be pouring your schoolmates endless glasses of peppermint water from the white pitcher. Don't forget that a month from now, on August 15th, it will be the Feast of the Assumption. You must take Holy Communion on that day to gladden the heart of your celestial mother, the Blessed Virgin. She will be pleased with her Patrick if you work hard to make her happy. You know that even on holiday, one mustn't forget to thank the Good Lord for all the wonderful times he gives us. Goodbye, my little Patrick. I embrace you with all my heart, Father Pachaud." The catechism classes were held on the top floor of a decrepit building at 4 Rue de l'Abbaye—which today contains opulent apartments—and in a meeting hall on Place de Furstenberg that has since become a luxury boutique. The faces have changed. I no longer recognize the neighborhood of my childhood, as Jacques Prévert or Father Pachaud would no longer recognize it.

On the other bank of the Seine were the mysteries of the Louvre courtyard, the two squares of the Carrousel, and the Tuileries, where my brother and I spent long afternoons. Black stone and leaves from the chestnut trees in the sun. The theater of greenery. The mountain of dead foliage against the foundation wall of the terrace under the Jeu de Paume. We assigned numbers to the alleyways. The empty fountain. The statue of Cain and Abel in one of the two bygone Carrousel squares. And the statue of La Fayette in the other square. The bronze lion in the Carrousel gardens. The green pair of scales against the wall of the Terrasse du Bord de l'Eau. The ceramic and coolness of the "lavatory" underneath the Terrasse des Feuillants. The groundskeepers. The rumble of the lawnmower engine, one sunny morning, on the grass near the fountain. The clock at the southern gate of the palace, its hands stopped for all eternity. And the fleur de lys branded on Milady's shoulder. We drew up family trees, my brother and I, and strained to establish a lineage between Saint Louis and Henry IV. At age eight, I was deeply impressed by a film: *The Greatest Show on Earth*. One scene in particular: At night, the train full of circus performers slams to a halt, blocked by an American car. Reflections of moonlight. The Médrano Circus. The orchestra played between acts. The clowns, Rhum, Alex, and Drena. Street carnivals. The one in Versailles, with bumper cars painted mauve, yellow, green, navy blue, pink . . . The street fair at Invalides with Jonas the Whale. Garages, their smell of shadows and gasoline. Penumbra. Sounds and voices faded into echoes.

Of my readings at the time (Jules Verne, Alexandre Dumas, Joseph Peyré, Conan Doyle, Selma Lagerlöf, Karl May, Mark Twain, James Oliver Curwood, Stevenson, *The Arabian Nights*, the comtesse de Ségur, Jack London), I especially remember *King Solomon's Mines*, the episode in which the young guide reveals his true identity as the king's son. And two book titles set me dreaming: *The Prisoner of Zenda* and *The Mystery Freighter*.

Our schoolmates on Rue du Pont-de-Lodi:

Pierre Do-Kiang, a Vietnamese whose parents ran a small hotel on Rue Grégoire-de-Tours. Zdanevich, half black, half Georgian, the son of the Georgian poet Iliazd. Other friends: Gérard, who lived above a garage in Deauville, on Avenue de la République. A certain Ronnie—I can't remember his face or where we met. We would play at his house near the Bois de Boulogne. I seem to recall that the moment we stepped through the front door, we were in London, one of those townhouses from Belgravia or Kensington. Later, when I read the Graham Greene story that became *The Fallen Idol,* I thought that Ronnie, about whom I knew nothing, could have been the protagonist.

Holidays in Deauville in a small cottage near Avenue de la République, with my father's girlfriend, Nathalie, the airline stewardess. My mother, on the rare occasions when she showed up, used it to entertain visiting friends, actors who were in a play at the Casino, and the Dutch friend from her youth, Joppie Van Allen. He belonged to the marquis de Cuevas's ballet company. Thanks to him, I saw a ballet that bowled me over, *La sonnambula*. One day I accompanied my father to the lobby of the Hôtel Royal, where he was to meet a Mme Stern, who, he said, owned a racing stable. What use could this Mme Stern have possibly been to him? Every Thursday, first thing in the afternoon, my brother and I would go buy *Tarzan* at the news dealer's opposite the church. It's hot. We are the only ones in the street. Sunlight and shadow dapple the sidewalk. The scent of privet . . .

In the summer of 1956, my brother and I lived in the cottage with my father and Nathalie, the airline stewardess. She had taken us on holiday, at Eastertime that same year, to a hotel in Villars-sur-Ollon. In Paris, one Sunday in 1954, my brother and I were standing in the wings of the Vieux-Colombier while my mother was onstage. A certain Suzy Prim, who played the lead, snapped coldly that we didn't belong here. Like many old hams, she didn't like children. I sent her a letter: "Dear Madam, I wish you a very bad Christmas." What had struck me about her was the look in her eyes, at once hard and anxious.

On Sundays, with my father, we would take the number 63 bus to the Bois de Boulogne. The lake and the floating dock from which one embarked for the miniature golf course and the Chalet des Iles . . . One evening, at the Bois, we were waiting for the bus home and my father dragged us into narrow Rue Adolphe-Yvon. He stopped in front of a private hotel and said, "I wonder who's living here now," as if he knew the place. I saw him in his office that evening, combing through the street directory. I was intrigued. A decade or so later, I learned that during the Occupation, 6 Rue Adolphe-Yvon, a private hotel that is no longer standing (I returned to that street in 1967 to verify the spot at which we'd stopped: it corresponded to number 6), was the address of the black market "Otto Bureau." And suddenly the stench of rot blends in with the smells of the riding clubs and dead leaves in the Bois. I also recall that sometimes on those afternoons, my brother, my father, and I would hop a random bus and ride it to the end of the line. Saint-Mandé. Porte de Gentilly . . .

In October 1956, I became a boarder at the Montcel school in Jouy-en-Josas. I've attended all the schools in Jouy-en-Josas. The first nights in the dormitory were hard and I often felt like crying. But soon I devised a trick to bolster my courage: I focused my attention on a fixed point, a kind of talisman. In this case, a little black plastic horse.

In February 1957, I lost my brother. One Sunday, my father and my Uncle Ralph came to collect me at the boarding school. On the road to Paris, my Uncle Ralph, who was driving, pulled the car over and stepped out, leaving me alone with my father. In the car, my father told me that my brother had died. I had spent the afternoon with him the previous Sunday, in our room on Quai de Conti. We had worked on our stamp collection. I had to return to school at five o'clock, and I'd explained that a theater troupe was going to put on a play for the students in the school's small auditorium. I will never forget the look on his face, that Sunday.

Apart from my brother, Rudy, his death, I don't believe that anything I'll relate here truly matters to me. I'm writing these pages the way one compiles a report or résumé, as documentation and to have done with a life that wasn't my own. It's just a simple film of deeds and facts. I have nothing to confess or elucidate and I have no interest in soul-searching or self-reflection. On the contrary, the more obscure and mysterious things remained, the more interesting I found them. I even looked for mystery where there was none. I lived through the events I'm recounting, up to the age of twenty-one, as if against a transparency—like in a cinematic process shot, when landscapes slide by in the background while the actors stand in place on a soundstage. I'd like to translate this impression, which many others have felt before me: everything paraded by like a transparency and I could not yet live my life.

I was a boarder at the Montcel school until

1960. Four years of military-style discipline. Every morning, flag salutes. Parade marches. Company, halt. Stand at attention. Evening inspections of the dormitories. Bullying by a few senior-year "captains" charged with maintaining "order." Electric clamor of the morning alarm. Showers in batches of thirty. Fitness trail. At ease. At attention. And the hours spent gardening, when, in a row, we raked up the dead leaves.

One of my classmates that year was named Safirstein. He was with me in the green dormitory. He told me that his father had been a medical student in Vienna when he was twenty. In 1938, at the time of the Anschluss, the Nazis had humiliated Vienna's Jews by forcing them to wash the sidewalks and paint the Star of David on the windows of their shops themselves. His father had suffered this bullying for a time, then fled Austria. One night, we decided to go explore inside the blockhouse at the far end of the park. This meant crossing the great lawn, and if one of the staff spotted us we could be severely punished. Safirstein had refused to join in this scouting expedition. The next day, my classmates ostracized him and called him a "chicken," with that garrison-style boorishness that emerges when "the men" are among themselves. Safirstein's father showed up unannounced at the college one afternoon. He wanted to talk to the entire dorm. He asked us nicely not to bully his son and to stop calling him "chicken." This way of handling things amazed my classmates, Safirstein included. We were all sitting around the table in the teachers' lounge. Safirstein was next to his father. Everyone made up in good spirits. I think his father gave us cigarettes. None of my schoolmates gave the incident any further thought. Not even Safirstein. But I had keenly felt the anxiousness of that man, who wondered if the nightmare he had suffered twenty years earlier wasn't starting up again for his son.

The Montcel school catered to the unloved, bastards, lost children. I remember a Brazilian who for a long while occupied the bed next to mine, who'd had no news of his parents for two years, as if they had left him in the checkroom of a forgotten station. Others were already smuggling blue jeans and sneaking past police roadblocks. Two of the students, two brothers, would even stand trial some twenty years later. Gilded youth, for the most part, but the gilding was tarnished, of poor alloy. Most of those fine young lads would have no future.

My readings at the time. Some books left their mark: *Fermina Márquez, The Penal Colony, Les Amours jaunes, The Sun Also Rises*. In other books, I rediscovered the fantastic character of the streets: *Marguerite de la nuit* by Pierre Mac Orlan, *Rien qu'une femme* by Francis Carco, *La Rue sans nom* by Marcel Aymé. In the college infirmaries, there were still some old novels lying around that had survived the last two wars, and that stood quietly on the shelves for fear someone might haul them down to the basement. I remember reading Bazin's *The Children of Alsace*. But mainly, I read the first "Livres de Poche" that had just been published, with their purple cardboard bindings. Good novels and bad, indiscriminately. Many have since gone out of print.

Among those books, several titles have retained their aroma: *La Rue du Chat-qui-Pêche, La Rose de Bratislava, Marion des neiges.*

On Sundays, strolls with my father and one of his cronies of the time, Stioppa. My father saw a lot of him. He wore a monocle and his hair was so thick with pomade that it left a stain when he rested his head against the sofa. He had no discernible profession. He lived in a boardinghouse on Avenue Victor-Hugo. Sometimes Stioppa, my father, and I would go walking in the Bois de Boulogne.

On another Sunday, my father took me to the boat show at the Quai Branly. We met a friend of his from before the war, "Paulo" Guerin. An aged young man wearing a blazer. I don't remember whether he was also visiting the show or manning a booth there. My father explained that Paulo Guerin never did anything but ride horses, drive around in fancy cars, and seduce the ladies. Let that be a lesson to me: yes, indeed, in life, you have to have your diplomas. That late afternoon, my father seemed pensive, as if he'd just met a ghost. Each time I've found myself on the Quai Branly, I've thought of this Paulo Guerin and his slightly stocky build, his pasty-looking face under swept-back brown hair. And the question remained forever unanswered: whatever could he have been doing at the boat show that Sunday, without his diplomas?

There was also a certain Charly d'Alton. It was especially with him and his old pal Lucien P. that my father tossed the phone back and forth like a rugby ball. His name reminded me of the Dalton Brothers in the comic books, and later I noticed that it was also the name of a friend of Alfred de Musset's. And a man my father always called by his surname, Rosen (or Rozen). This Rosen (or Rozen) was the spitting image of the actor David Niven. I seem to recall that during the Spanish Civil War, he enlisted on the side of Franco. He could sit silently on the couch for hours. Even in my father's absence. Even at night, I imagine. He was part of the furniture.

Sometimes my father came with me on Monday mornings to the Rotonde at the Porte d'Orléans. That's where I would catch the bus that took me back to school. We got up at six o'clock, and my father used the time before the bus arrived to hold appointments in the cafés around the Porte d'Orléans, lit with neon on those winter mornings when it was still pitch black outside. Hiss of the percolators. The people he saw there were different from the ones he met at the Claridge or the Grand Hôtel. They spoke in low voices. Stall hawkers, men with the ruddy complexion of traveling salesmen or the sly demeanor of provincial clerks. What did he want with them, exactly? They sported rural names like Quintard, Chevreau, Picard . . .

One Sunday morning, we took a taxi to the Bastille neighborhood. My father had the driver stop about twenty times in front of apartment houses on Boulevard Voltaire, Avenue de la République, Boulevard Richard-Lenoir . . . Each time, he left an envelope with the concierge. A notice to former shareholders of a defunct company whose stock certificates he had unearthed? Something like the Union Minière

Indochinoise? On another Sunday, he dropped off his envelopes along Boulevard Pereire.

Sometimes, on Saturday evenings, we went to visit an elderly couple, the Facons, who lived in a minuscule apartment on Rue du Ruisseau, behind Montmartre. On the wall of the tiny living room, exhibited in a frame, was the military medal M. Facon had been awarded in World War I. He was a former printer who loved literature. He gave me a handsomely bound edition of Saint-Pol Roux's book of poems *La Rose et les épines du chemin*. Under what circumstances had my father met him?

I also remember a certain Léon Grunwald. He came to lunch with my father several times a week. Tall, with wavy gray hair, face like a spaniel's, drooping eyes and shoulders. Much later, I was surprised to find a trace of the man in Jesús Ynfante's book on the "Broglie Affair": In 1968, the president of a company called Matesa "was seeking financing to the tune of fifteen to twenty million dollars." He had got in touch with Léon Grunwald, "who had helped arrange the primary financing to Luxembourg." A memorandum of understanding was signed by "Jean de Broglie, Raoul de Léon, and Léon Grunwald"; if the loan went through, they stood to earn a commission of five hundred thousand dollars. According to what I read, Grunwald had died in the interim. From exhaustion? It's true that these kinds of people have demanding jobs and spend many a sleepless night. By day, they schedule countless meetings with one another to try to sign their "memoranda of understanding."

I would like to breathe purer air, my head is spinning, but still I recall several of my father's "appointments." One late morning I had accompanied him to the Champs-Elysées. We were welcomed by a short, bald, very vivacious man, in a cupboard-sized office where we could barely find room to sit. I thought he was one of the seven dwarves. He kept his voice down, as if he wasn't supposed to be there.

Normally, my father held his "appointments" in the lobby of the Claridge, where he took me on Sundays. One afternoon, I stayed to the side while he conferred in undertones with an Englishman. He tried to grab a sheet of paper the Englishman had just initialed, but the latter snatched it away too quickly. What "memorandum of understanding" could this have been? My father had an office in a large, ochre-colored building at 1 Rue Lord-Byron, where he headed the Société Africaine d'Entreprise, along with a secretary named Lucienne Wattier, a former model whom he addressed with the familiar *tu*. This is one of my first memories of the Paris streets: walking up Rue Balzac, then turning right onto Rue Lord-Byron. One could also reach this office by entering the Normandie cinema on the Champs-Elysées side and following a tangle of hallways.

On the mantelpiece of my father's room were several volumes of "maritime law," which he was studying. Something to do with a cigar-shaped oil tanker he wanted to have built. My father's Corsican lawyers: Maître Mariani, whom we would visit at home, and Maître Vizzavona. Sunday walks with my father and an

Italian engineer, who held a patent for "pressure ovens." My father became close friends with a certain M. Held, "water diviner," who always wore a pocket watch on a chain. One evening, on the stairs, my father said something that I didn't fully grasp at the time — one of the rare instances when he opened up to me: "One should never neglect the little details . . . Unfortunately, I've always neglected the little details."

In those years, 1957 and 1958, another of his cronies appeared, a certain Jacques Chatillon. I saw him again twenty years later, by which point he was calling himself James B. Chatillon. At the start of the Occupation he had married the granddaughter of a merchant whose secretary he was, and during that time he had been a horse trader in Neuilly. He sent me a letter in which he talked about my father: "Don't be upset that he died alone. Your father didn't mind being alone. He had great imagination — though to be honest, entirely devoted to his business — that he nourished carefully and that nourished his mind. He was never alone, for he was always 'conspiring' with some scheme or other, and that's what gave him that strange air that many found so unnerving. He was curious about everything, even things he didn't agree with. He managed to give an impression of calm, but he could easily turn violent. When something annoyed him, his eyes would flash. He opened them wide, instead of keeping them hidden under his heavy eyelids. Above all, he was a dilettante. What always shocked his contacts the most was his reluctance to speak, to make himself clear. He would mumble a few allusions . . . punctuated with one or two hand gestures and a 'there you have it' . . . then clear his throat once or twice to top it off. Along with his reluctance to speak went his reluctance to set things down on paper, which he explained away as being due to his illegible handwriting."

James B. Chatillon wanted me to write the biography of a friend of his, a Corsican mobster named Jean Sartore, who had just died and who'd associated with the Rue Lauriston gang and its boss, Lafont, during the Occupation. "I sincerely regret that you couldn't write Jean Sartore's memoirs, but you're wrong to think he was an old friend of Lafont's. He used Lafont as a screen for his gold and currency smuggling, since the Germans were after him even more than the French. That said, he knew plenty about the Lauriston bunch."

In 1969, after my second novel came out, he had phoned me and left a name and number where I could reach him. It was in care of a M. de Varga, who was later implicated in Jean de Broglie's murder. I remember one Sunday when we walked around Mont Valérien, my father and I and this Chatillon, a stocky, brown-haired fellow, with lively black eyes under pale lids. He drove us there in an old Bentley with collapsed leather seats—the only asset he had left. After a while, he had to part with that, too, and would come to the Quai de Conti on a moped. He was deeply devout. I once asked him, provocatively, "What good is religion, anyway?" He had given

me a biography of Pope Pius XI with this in-
scription: "For Patrick, so that he might learn
'what good religion is' . . ."

Often my father and I were alone on Saturday evenings. We saw movies at the Champs-
Elysées and the Gaumont Palace. One afternoon
in June, we were walking—I don't remember
why—on Boulevard Rochechouart. The sun
was very strong and we retreated into the dark-
ness of a small movie house, the Delta. At the
George V cinema, there was a documentary on
the Nuremberg Trials, *Hitler's Executioners:* at age
thirteen, I discovered images of the extermina-
tion camps. Something changed for me that day.
And what did my father think? We never talked
about it, not even as we left the theater.

On summer nights we would get ice cream at
Ruc or the Régence. Dinner at L'Alsacienne on
the Champs-Elysées, or at the Chinese restaurant on Rue du Colisée. In the evening, on the
dark red leather-covered record player, we'd listen to test pressings of vinyl records he wanted
to put on the market. And on his bedside table, I

remember one book: *How to Make Friends,* which today helps me understand his solitude. One Monday morning during the holidays, I heard steps on the inner staircase leading to the fifth floor, where my room was. Then voices in the large bathroom next door. Bailiffs were carting away all of my father's suits, shirts, and shoes. What ploy had kept them from repossessing the furniture?

Summer vacations in 1958 and 1959 in Mégève, where I was alone with a young girl, an art student who watched over me like a big sister. The Hôtel de la Résidence was closed and looked abandoned. We crossed through the unlit lobby to use the pool. After 5 P.M., an Italian orchestra played around that pool. A doctor and his wife had rented us two rooms in their house. Strange couple. The wife, a brunette, seemed crazy. They had adopted a girl my age, sweet like all unloved children, with whom I spent afternoons in the deserted classrooms of the nearby school. Beneath the summer sun, a smell of grass and asphalt.

Easter holidays, 1959, with a schoolmate who took me to Monte Carlo, so I wouldn't be left alone at the boarding school; we stayed with his grandmother, the marquise de Polignac. She was American. I later found out that she was a cousin of Harry Crosby, the publisher of Lawrence and Joyce in Paris, who killed himself at age thirty. She owned a black car with front-wheel drive. Her husband dealt in champagne, and before the war they had socialized with Joachim von Ribbentrop, when he too was a champagne salesman. But my friend's father was a former Resistance member and a Trotskyite. He wrote a book about Yugoslavian Communism with a preface by Sartre. I'd learn all this later. In Monte Carlo, I spent entire afternoons at the marquise's, leafing through photo albums she'd put together, starting in the 1920s, illustrating the easy, carefree life she and her husband had led. She wanted to teach me how to drive and gave me the wheel of her 15 HP on a sharply twisting road. I missed a turn and we nearly went hurtling into the void. She brought

us to Nice, her grandson and me, to see Luis
Mariano at the Pinder Circus.

Stays in Bournemouth, England, in 1959 and
1960. Verlaine once lived in that area: scattered
red cottages amid the foliage and white villas
along the seafront . . . I don't expect to return to
France. I've had no word from my mother. And I
think it suits my father for me to stay in England
longer than planned. The family I'm lodging
with can't keep me any longer. So I show up at
a hotel reception desk with the three thousand
francs I possess, and they let me sleep free of
charge in an unused sitting room on the ground
floor. Then the headmaster of the school where
I study English in the mornings puts me up in a
kind of broom closet under the stairs. I run away
to London. I arrive at Waterloo Station that
evening. I cross Waterloo Bridge. I'm terrified
at being alone in this city that seems so much
bigger than Paris. From a red phone booth in
Trafalgar Square, I call my father collect. I try
to hide my panic. He doesn't sound very surprised to learn I'm in London on my own. He

wishes me good luck, in an indifferent voice. At a small hotel in Bloomsbury, they agree to give me a room, even though I'm a minor. But just for one night. And the next day, I try my luck at another hotel, near the Marble Arch. There, too, they look the other way at my being fifteen and give me a tiny room. This was still the England of the Teddy boys and the London where seventeen-year-old Christine Keeler had just arrived from the suburbs. Later, I learned that she worked, that same summer, as a waitress in a small Greek restaurant on Baker Street, right near the Turkish place where I used to eat in the evening before my anxious walks down Oxford Street. "And De Quincey sipping / Sweet opium chaste and poisonous / Brooded on his unhappy Anne . . ."

One night in September 1959, with my mother and one of her friends, in the Koutoubia, an Arab restaurant on Rue des Ecoles. It's late. The restaurant is empty. It's still summer. The weather is hot. The street door is wide open. In those strange years of my adolescence, Algiers was an extension of Paris, and Paris was washed by the waves and echoes of Algiers, as if the sirocco blew over the trees in the Tuileries, bringing sand from the desert and beaches . . . In Algiers as in Paris, the same Vespas, the same movie posters, the same songs in the café jukeboxes, the same Renault Dauphines in the streets. The same summer in Algiers as along the Champs-Elysées. That evening at the Koutoubia, which city were we in? Some time later, they bombed the Koutoubia. One evening in Saint-Germain-des-Prés—or was it Algiers?— they bombed the Jack Romoli menswear shop.

That autumn of 1959, my mother was in a play at the Théâtre Fontaine. On the Saturday evenings when we could leave school, I sometimes did my homework in the theater director's office. And I walked around. I discovered the Pigalle neighborhood, less rustic than Saint-Germain-des-Prés, somewhat rougher than the Champs-Elysées. It was there, on Rue Fontaine,

Place Blanche, Rue Frochot, that I first brushed against the mysteries of Paris and, without realizing it, began dreaming of a life for myself.

On the Quai de Conti, two newcomers were living in the apartment: Robert Fly, an old friend of my father's, who served as his chauffeur and took him everywhere in a Citroën DS 19, and Robert Car, a costume designer my mother had gotten to know on the set of Max Pécas's film *Le Cercle vicieux,* in which she played the part of a rich and disturbing foreigner, the mistress of a young painter.

In January 1960, I ran away from school because I was infatuated with a certain Kiki Daragane, whom I'd met at my mother's. After walking to the hangars of the Villacoublay airfield, then reaching Saint-Germain-des-Prés by bus and metro, I happened to run into Kiki Daragane at the café Malafosse, where Rue Bonaparte meets the quay. She was with some art student friends. They advised me to go back home. I rang at my door, but there was no answer. My father must have been out with Robert Fly in the DS 19. My mother was away, as usual. I needed a place to sleep. I went back to the boarding school by metro and bus, after begging a little money off Kiki and her friends. The principal agreed to keep me until June. But at the end of the school year, I was to be expelled.

On my rare days out, my father and Robert Fly would sometimes take me along on their perambulations. They crisscrossed the Ile-de-France. They met with notaries and visited an array of properties. They stopped at rustic inns. Apparently my father, for some pressing reason, wanted to "get out of town." In Paris, long confabulations between Robert Fly and my father, at the back of the office at 73 Boulevard Haussmann, where I would join them. Robert Fly sported a blond mustache. Apart from driving the DS 19, I have no idea what he did. Now and then, he told me, he took a "side trip" to Pigalle, and he would return home to the Quai de Conti at seven in the morning. Robert Car turned a bedroom of the apartment into a dressmaking studio. My father nicknamed him Truffaldino, after a character in the commedia dell'arte. In the 1940s, it had been Robert Car who dressed the first transvestites: La Zambella, Lucky Sarcel, Zizi Moustic.

I accompanied my father to Rue Christophe-Colomb, where he visited a new "crony," a certain Morawski, in a small private hotel at number 12 or 14. I would wait for him, pacing back and forth under the leaves of the chestnut trees. It was early spring. My mother was in a play at the Théâtre des Arts, directed by a Mme Alexandra Roubé-Jansky. The play was called *Women Want to Know*. It was by a silk manufacturer from Lyon and his girlfriend and they'd underwritten the entire production, renting out the theater and paying the actors out of pocket. Every evening they played to an empty hall. The only spectators were a few friends of the silk manufacturer's. The director wisely counseled the manufacturer not to invite the critics, on the pretext that they were "mean" . . .

On the last Sunday evening before summer holidays, Robert Fly and my father drove me to the Montcel school in the DS 19 and waited while I packed my suitcase. After stashing it in the trunk of the DS, I left Jouy-en-Josas for good via the westbound highway.

Apparently, they wanted to keep me away from Paris. In September 1960, I was enrolled in the Saint-Joseph de Thônes secondary school, in the mountains of the Haute-Savoie. A man called Jacques Gérin and his wife, Stella, my father's sister, were my unofficial guardians. They lived in a rented white house with green shutters in Veyrier, on the edge of Lake Annecy. But apart from the rare Sundays when I was let out of school for a few hours, there wasn't much they could do for me.

"Jacky" Gérin dabbled "in textiles." He was originally from Lyon, a bohemian, fond of classical music, skiing, and expensive cars. Stella Gérin carried on a correspondence with the Geneva lawyer Pierre Jaccoud, who had been convicted of murder and was then serving time. When Jaccoud was released, she went to see him in Geneva. I later met him with her, at the bar of the Mövenpick, around 1963. He spoke to me of literature, particularly Mallarmé.

In Paris, Jacky Gérin served as front man for

Uncle Ralph, my father's younger brother: the
so-called Etablissements Gérin, 74 Rue d'Hauteville, was in fact run by Uncle Ralph. I was never
able to clarify the exact nature of that Etablissements Gérin, a sort of warehouse where Uncle
Ralph had an office and sold "equipment." Several years later, I asked him why the business
was named Gérin and not Modiano, after him.
He answered in his Paris accent: "Gotta understand, kid, Italian-sounding names didn't really
cut it after the war . . ."

On my last holiday afternoons, I read *The
Devil in the Flesh* and *Witches' Sabbath* on the
small beach at Veyrier-du-Lac. A few days before classes started, my father sent me a harsh
letter, the type of letter that could easily dis-
hearten a boy about to be locked away in boarding school. Was he trying to assuage his con-
science by convincing himself he was rightly
abandoning a delinquent to his fate? "ALBERT
RODOLPHE MODIANO 15 QUAI DE CONTI Paris
VI, September 8, 1960. I'm returning the letter you sent me from Saint-Lô. I must tell you

that, reading it, I did not believe for one second that your desire to return to Paris had anything to do with studying for entrance exams. That is why I decided you should leave the following morning, on the 9 o'clock train to Annecy. I expect a report about your conduct at this new school and I can only hope for your sake that it is exemplary. I had intended to come visit you in Geneva. Under the circumstances, this trip now seems pointless. ALBERT MODIANO."

My mother blew through Annecy, just long enough to buy me two items for my school outfit: a gray smock and a used pair of shoes with crepe soles that would last me a good ten years and never leak. She left well before evening. It is always painful to see a child return to boarding school, knowing he'll be a prisoner there. One would like to hold him back. Did that cross her mind? It seems I found no favor in her eyes. And besides, she was about to leave on a long trip to Spain.

Still September. New school year, Sunday evening. The first days at the Collège Saint-

Joseph were hard for me. But I quickly got used
to it. I had already spent four years in boarding
schools. My schoolmates in Thônes were mainly
of peasant origin, and I preferred them to the
gilt-edged hooligans of Montcel.

Unfortunately, our reading was monitored.
In 1962, I would be suspended for a few days
for reading *Ripening Seed* by Colette. Thanks to
my French teacher, Father Accambray, I would
be granted "special" permission to read *Madame
Bovary*, which was forbidden to the others. I've
kept the copy of the book in which they wrote,
"Approved—Junior year," with the signature of
Father Janin, the school principal. Father Accambray recommended one of Mauriac's novels
to me, *The Unknown Sea*, which I greatly enjoyed,
especially the ending—so much so that I still remember the final phrase: ". . . as in the black
dawns of yesteryear." He also suggested *Les Dé-
racinés* by Barrès. Had he sensed that what I was
missing was a village in Sologne or the Valois, or
rather, my dream version of them? My bedside
books in the dormitory: Pavese's *This Business of*

Living, which they hadn't thought to ban. *Manon Lescaut. Les Filles du feu. Wuthering Heights. Diary of a Country Priest.*

A few hours of liberty once a month, and then the Sunday evening bus would take me back to school. I waited for it at the foot of the large tree, near the town hall of Veyrier-du-Lac. I often had to make the trip standing, because of all the farmers returning home after a Sunday in town. Night was falling. We drove past the chateau of Menthon-Saint-Bernard, the small cemetery of Alex and the one where the Resistance heroes of the Glières Plateau were buried. Those Sunday evening buses and the trains between Annecy and Paris were as packed as during the Occupation. Moreover, they were basically the same buses and trains.

The Generals' Putsch in Algiers, which I followed in the dorm on my little transistor radio, thinking I should take advantage of the widespread panic to break out of school. But order was restored in France by the following Sunday evening.

The nightlights in the dormitory. Returning to the dormitory after the holidays. The first
night was the worst. You would wake up and not
know where you were. The nightlights brought
it all back brutally. Lights out at 9 P.M. The bed
was too small. The sheets weren't washed for
months and smelled bad. So did our clothes. Up
in the morning at 6:15. Cursory wash, in cold
water, at sinks that were ten yards long: troughs
topped with a row of spigots. Study. Breakfast.
Unsweetened coffee in a metal bowl. No but-
ter. During morning recess, in the covered playground, we huddled together to read a copy of
the newspaper *L'Echo Liberté*. A slice of dry bread
and a square of dark chocolate handed out at
4 P.M. Polenta for dinner. I was starving. I felt
dizzy. One day, some schoolmates and I yelled at
the bursar, Father Bron, telling him there wasn't
enough to eat. Class walks around Thônes on
Thursday afternoons. I took the opportunity to
buy *Les Lettres françaises*, *Arts*, and *Les Nouvelles
littéraires* at the village newsstand. I read them
cover to cover. All these weeklies piled up on my

nightstand. Recess after lunch, when I listened to the radio. In the distance, behind the trees, the monotonous whine of the sawmill. Endless rainy days under the playground roof. The row of stand-up toilets with doors that didn't stay shut. Evening Benediction in the chapel before returning to the dormitory, in line. Six months of snow. I've always felt there was something touching and benevolent about that snow. And a song that year, on the transistor radio: *Non je ne me souviens plus du nom du bal perdu* . . .

During the school year, I occasionally received a letter from my mother, from Andalusia. Most of her letters were sent care of the Gérins in Veyrier-du-Lac, except for two or three that went to my school. Letters sent and received had to be unsealed, and Janin, the canon, deemed it odd, this husbandless mother in Andalusia. She wrote to me from Seville: "You should start reading Montherlant. I think you could learn a lot from him. My boy, take this to heart. Please, do it, read Montherlant. You'll find him full of good advice. How a young man should act around women, for instance. Really, you could learn a lot by reading Montherlant's *The Girls*." Her vehemence surprised me—my mother had never read a word of Montherlant in her life. It was a friend of hers, the journalist Jean Cau, who had prompted her to give me that advice, which I still find puzzling: did he really think Montherlant should be my guide in sexual matters? In any event, I innocently began reading *The Girls*. Personally, I prefer his *Le Fichier parisien*. In 1961, my mother inadvertently sent me another letter that raised the canon's eyebrows. This one contained press clippings about a comedy, *Le Signe de Kikota*, in which she was touring with Fernand Gravey.

Christmas 1960, in Rome with my father and his new girlfriend, a high-strung Italian, twenty years his junior, hair the color of straw and face like a poor man's Mylène Demongeot. A photo taken on New Year's Eve in a nightclub near the Via Veneto perfectly captures the visit. I look pensive and, forty years later, I wonder what I was doing there. To cheer myself up, I pretend

the photo is a composite. The ersatz Mylène Demongeot wanted to get a religious annulment of
her first marriage. One afternoon, I accompanied her to the Vatican to see a Monsignor Pen-
dola. Despite his cassock and the inscribed picture of the pope on his desk, he looked just like
the hucksters my father used to meet at the Claridge. My father seemed startled, that Christmas,
by the severe chilblains on my hands.

Back to boarding school, until summer vaca-
tion. At the beginning of July, my mother returned from Spain. I went to meet her at Geneva
Airport. She had dyed her hair brown. She
moved in with the Gérins in Veyrier-du-Lac.
She didn't have a cent. Barely a pair of shoes to
her name. The stay in Spain had not been suc-
cessful, and yet she had lost none of her arro-
gance. She told us, with chin raised, "sublime"
stories of Andalusia and bullfighters. But beneath the theatricality and fantasy, she had a
heart of stone.

My father came to spend a few days in the
area, accompanied by the marquis Philippe

de D., with whom he had business dealings. A
large, blustery blond with a mustache, trailed by
his brunette mistress. He borrowed my father's
passport to go to Switzerland. They were of
similar build, with the same mustache and the
same corpulence, and D. had lost his papers
when he'd fled Tunisia following the military
action in Bizerte. I can still see myself with my
father, Philippe de D., and the brunette mistress
at a sidewalk table at Père Bise in Talloires, and
once again I wonder what I was doing there. In
August, my mother and I left for Knokke-le-
Zoute, where a family she'd been friends with
before the war took us into their small villa.
It was kind of them; otherwise we would have
had to sleep under the stars or at the Salvation
Army. Spoiled, boorish teenagers hung out at
the go-kart track. Industrialists from Ghent
with the casual manners of yachtsmen greeted
each other in their deep voices, in a French to
which they labored to give English inflections. A
friend from my mother's youth, who looked like
an overripe delinquent, ran a nightclub behind

the dunes, near Ostend. Then I returned alone to the Haute-Savoie. My mother went back to Paris. Another school year began for me at the Collège Saint-Joseph.

Break for All Saints' Day, 1961. Rue Royale, Annecy, in the rain and melting snow. In the bookstore window, Moravia's novel *Boredom*, with its belly band: "And Its Relief: Eros." During those gray holidays, I read *Crime and Punishment*, and it was my sole comfort. I came down with scabies. I went to see a doctor, whose name I'd found in the Annecy phone book. She was shocked at my weakened state. She asked, "Don't you have parents?" At her solicitude and maternal kindness, I had to force myself not to break down in sobs.

In January 1962, a letter from my mother that, luckily, did not fall into the hands of Father Janin: "I didn't call you this week, I wasn't home. Friday night I was at a cocktail party that Litvak threw on the set of his film. I was also at the premiere of Truffaut's film *Jules and Jim*, and this evening I'm going to see the Calderón play at TNP. . . . I'm thinking of you and know how hard you work. Be brave, my dearest boy. I'm still not sorry I turned down the play with Bourvil. I'd have been too miserable playing such a vulgar role. I hope to find something else. My son, don't think I've forgotten you but I have so little time to send care packages."

In February 1962, I took advantage of the Shrove Tuesday break and hopped the crowded train to Paris, running a high fever. I was hoping my parents, seeing me so ill, would let me stay in Paris for a while. My mother had moved into the third-floor apartment, where the only remaining furniture was a sagging couch. My father was living on the fourth floor with the ersatz Mylène Demongeot. At my mother's, I saw the journalist Jean Cau, who had a bodyguard because of the OAS assassination plots. Sartre's former secretary was an odd duck, with his lynxlike face and his obsession with bullfighters. When I was fourteen, I'd convinced him that the son of Alexandre Stavisky, under a false name, was at school with me and had told me his father was still alive somewhere in South America. Cau had arrived at my school in his 4 CV, desperate to meet "Stavisky's son" and come away with a scoop. That winter, I also saw Jean Normand (alias Jean Duval), a friend of my mother's who had recommended pulp novels to me when I was eleven. At the time, 1956, I couldn't have known that he'd just got out of prison. There was also Mireille Ourousov. She slept in the living room on the old couch. A brunette of twenty-eight or thirty. My mother had met her in Andalusia. She was married to a Russian, Eddy Ourousov, nick-named "the Consul" because he drank as much as the hero of Malcolm Lowry's novel—cuba libres. The two of them ran a small hotel-bar in Torremolinos. She was French. She told me that when she was seventeen, on the morning she was scheduled to take the baccalaureate exams, her alarm didn't go off and she slept until noon. It was somewhere around the Landes. At night my mother would be out, and I stayed home with Mireille Ourousov. She couldn't sleep on that small, sagging couch. And I had a large

bed . . . One morning, I was with her in Place
de l'Odéon. A gypsy read our palms, under the
arcades of the Cour du Commerce Saint-André.
Mireille Ourousov said she'd be curious to know
me in ten years.

Return to Thônes in drab March. The bishop
of Annecy paid a formal visit to the school. We
kissed his ring. Speeches. Mass. And I received
a letter from my father that the canon Janin
never opened and that, if it had had any basis
in reality, would have been the letter of a model
father to his model son: "May 2, 1962. My dear
Patrick, We should tell each other everything
with complete honesty; it's the one and only way
to keep from becoming strangers, as sadly hap-
pens in too many families. I'm glad you've con-
fided in me about the problem now facing you:
what you'll do later on, what direction to take in
life. You've explained to me, on the one hand,
that you understand diplomas are necessary to
obtain a good position, and on the other, that
you need to express yourself by writing books
or plays and would like to devote yourself fully

to this. Most of the men who have enjoyed the greatest literary success, apart from a few rare exceptions, had been brilliant students. You can cite as many examples as I can: Sartre would probably never have written some of his books if he hadn't pursued his studies through an advanced degree in philosophy. Claudel wrote *The Satin Slipper* when he was a young embassy attaché in Japan, after graduating with top honors from 'Sciences Po.' Romain Gary, who won the Prix Goncourt, is another alumnus of 'Sciences Po,' and a consul in the United States." He wanted me to become an agricultural engineer. He considered it an up-and-coming profession. If he attached so much importance to schooling, it's because he himself hadn't had any and was a little like those mobsters who send their daughters off to be educated by the "sisters." He spoke with a slight Paris accent—the accent of Cité d'Hauteville and Rue des Petits-Hôtels and also the Cité Trévise, where you can hear the fountain murmuring in the silence beneath the trees. Once in a while he used slang. But he could inspire trust in potential investors, for he looked like a pleasant, reserved fellow, tall and soberly dressed.

I took my baccalaureate exam in Annecy. This would be my only diploma. Paris in July. My father. My mother. She was in a revival of *Les Portes claquent* at the Daunou. The ersatz Mylène Demongeot. The Parc Monceau, where I read newspaper articles about the end of the Algerian War. The Bois de Boulogne. I discovered Céline's *Journey to the End of the Night*. I was happy when I walked the streets of Paris by myself. One Sunday in August, in the southeastern part of town—Boulevard Jourdan and Boulevard Kellerman, a neighborhood I'd later come to know so well—I learned from a news dealer's display about Marilyn Monroe's suicide.

The month of August in Annecy. Claude. She turned twenty that summer of 1962. She worked for a dressmaker in Lyon. Then she became a "temp" model. Then, in Paris, a full-time model. Then she married a Sicilian prince and went to live in Rome, where time stops forever.

Robert. He scandalized Annecy by loudly pro-
claiming himself a "queen." He was a pariah in
that provincial town. That same summer of 1962,
he was twenty-six. He reminded me of Divine
in Genet's *Our Lady of the Flowers.* When very
young, Robert had been the boyfriend of the
Belgian baron Jean L. during the latter's stay at
the Hôtel Impérial Palace in Annecy—the same
baron whose shill my mother had known in Antwerp in 1939. I saw Robert again in 1973. One
Sunday evening, in Geneva, we were driving in
his car across the Pont des Bergues, and he was
so drunk that we nearly toppled into the Rhone.
He died in 1980. His face bore the marks of a
beating and the police arrested a friend of his. I
read about it in the papers: "The real death of a
larger than life character."

A girl, Marie. In the summer, she took the
bus in Annecy, as did I, on Place de la Gare, at
seven in the evening after work. She was going
home to Veyrier-du-Lac. I met her on that bus.
She was barely older than I and already working
as a typist. On her days off, we would rendez-

vous at the small beach in Veyrier-du-Lac. She read Maurois's *A History of England*. And photo comics that I'd buy for her before joining her on the beach.

The kids my age who spent time at the Sporting or the Taverne, and who are now gone with the wind: Jacques L., called "the Marquis," the son of a *milicien* who'd been shot for treason in August 1944 at Grand-Bornand. Pierre Fournier, who carried a knobbed walking stick. And those who belonged to the generation of the Algerian War: Claude Brun, Zazie, Paulo Hervieu, Rosy, La Yeyette, who had been Pierre Brasseur's mistress. Dominique the brunette with her black leather jacket passed beneath the arcades, and they said she lived "off her charms" in Geneva . . . Claude Brun and friends. A gang of *vitelloni*. Their cult film was *The American Beauty*. Returning from the Algerian War, they had bought secondhand MGs. They took me to a "floodlit" football match. One of them had bet he could seduce the prefect's wife inside of two weeks and take her to the Grand Hôtel in Verdun, and he'd won; another was the lover of a rich and very pretty woman, the widow of a local notable, who in winter frequented the bridge club on the first floor of the Casino.

I used to take the bus to Geneva, where sometimes I saw my father. We had lunch in an Italian restaurant with a man called Picard. In the afternoons, he held appointments. Curious Geneva of the very early sixties. Algerians spoke in low voices in the lobby of the Hôtel du Rhône. I would walk around the historic part of town. They said that Dominique the brunette, on whom I had a crush, was working in a nightclub at 58 Rue Glacis-de-Rive. On the way back, the bus crossed the border at sunset, without stopping for customs.

In the summer of 1962, my mother came through Annecy on tour, playing in Sacha Guitry's *Ecoutez bien, messieurs* at the Casino, with Jean Marchat and Michel Flamme, a typical blond "good-looking boy" who wore leopard-print bathing briefs. He took us for refreshments at the bar of the Sporting. A Sunday walk along the Pâquier gardens with Claude when the holidays were over. Autumn already. We walked past the prefecture, where a girlfriend of hers worked. Annecy turned back into a provincial town. In the Pâquier, we came across an old Armenian, always on his own; according to Claude, he was a wealthy businessman who gave lots of money to girls and paupers. And Jacky Gérin's gray automobile, with body by Allemano, circled slowly around the lake for all eternity. I will keep on reciting these moments, without nostalgia but in a rush. It's not my fault if the words jumble together. I have to move quickly, before I lose heart.

That September, in Paris, I started at the Lycée Henri-IV, in the preparatory *classe de philosophie,* as a full boarder, even though my parents' apartment was only a few hundred yards from the school. I'd been living in dormitories for the past six years. I had known harsher discipline in my other schools, but I had never been as miserable as I was at Henri-IV. Especially at the hour when I watched the day students leave by the main porch and fan out into the streets.

I don't remember my fellow boarders very well. I seem to recall three boys from Sarreguemines who were prepping for the Ecole Normale Supérieure. A Martinican in my class was usually with them. There was another student who always smoked a pipe, and constantly wore a gray smock and carpet slippers. They said he hadn't been outside the school walls in three years. I also vaguely recall my bunkmate, a small red-haired kid, whom I spotted from afar two or three years later, on Boulevard Saint-

Michel, in a private's uniform in the rain . . .
After lights out, a watchman came through the
dormitories, lantern in hand, to make sure every
bed was occupied. It was the fall of 1962, but
also the nineteenth century and, perhaps, a time
still farther in the past as well.

My father came only once to visit me in that
institution. The headmaster gave me permission to wait for him on the entrance porch. That
headmaster had a lovely name: Adonis Del-
fosse. The silhouette of my father, there, on the
porch—but I can't make out his face, as if his
presence in those medieval monastic surround-
ings seemed unreal. The silhouette of a tall man
with no head. I don't remember if there was a
parlor. I think we spoke in a room on the first
floor, the library or perhaps the social hall. We
were alone, sitting at a table, opposite each
other. I accompanied him back down to the
porch. He walked away across Place du Pan-
théon. He'd once told me that he, too, had hung
around that part of town when he was eighteen.
He had just enough money to buy himself a café

au lait and a couple of croissants at the Dupont-Latin, in lieu of a proper meal. In those days, he had a shadow on his lung. I close my eyes and imagine him walking up Boulevard Saint-Michel, among the well-behaved *lycée* pupils and the students belonging to Action Française. *His* Latin Quarter was the one of Violette Nozière. He must have run across her many times on the boulevard. Violette, "the pretty schoolgirl from the Lycée Fénelon who raised bats in her desk."

My father married the ersatz Mylène Demongeot. They lived on the fourth floor, right above my mother. The two floors formed a single apartment, from the time when my parents lived together. In 1962, the two apartments hadn't yet been separated. Behind a boarded-up doorway, there was still the interior staircase that my father had built in 1947, when he'd begun renting the third floor. The ersatz Mylène Demongeot was not keen on me being a day pupil or continuing to see my father. After I'd spent two months as a boarder, he sent me this letter: "ALBERT RODOLPHE MODIANO 15 QUAI

DE CONTI Paris VI. You came up this morning at 9:15 to inform me that you had decided not to return to school as long as I did not reverse my decision to keep you there as a boarder. At around 12:30, you again confirmed the above. Your behavior is beyond disgraceful. If you think that such pathetic attempts at blackmail will win me over, you've got another think coming. Therefore I strongly advise you, for your own sake, to go back to school tomorrow morning, with a note for your headmaster excusing your absence due to a cold. I must warn you in no uncertain terms that if you do not, you will regret it. You are seventeen, you are still a minor, I am your father, and I'm responsible for your education. I intend to have a word with your headmaster. Albert Modiano."

My mother had no money and no theatrical engagements that October of 1962. And my father was threatening to discontinue my child support unless I moved back into the dormitory. Thinking about it today, I can't imagine I cost him very much: just modest room and board.

But I remember seeing him in the late 1950s, so utterly "broke" that he had to borrow the few francs my grandfather sometimes sent me from Belgium out of his retirement pension. I felt closer to him than to my own parents.

I continued to be "on strike" from the boarding school. One afternoon, my mother and I were walking in the Tuileries; we didn't have a cent. As a last resort, she decided to ask her friend Suzanne Flon for help. We went to Suzanne Flon's on foot, having not even enough change for two metro tickets. Suzanne Flon welcomed us into her apartment on Avenue George-V with its superposed balconies. It was like being on a cruise ship. We stayed for dinner. In melodramatic tones, my mother laid out our "misfortunes," her feet planted firmly, with theatrical and peremptory gestures. Suzanne Flon listened indulgently, deploring our situation. She offered to write my father a letter. She gave my mother some money.

Over the following months, my father had to resign himself to my finally leaving the dormitories where I'd lived since age eleven. He made appointments to see me in cafés. And he trotted out his standard grievances against my mother and against me. I could never establish a bond between us. At each meeting, I was reduced to begging him for a fifty-franc bill, which he would give me very grudgingly and which I'd bring home to my mother. On certain days, I brought nothing home, which provoked furious outbursts from her. Soon—around the time I turned eighteen and in the years following—I started trying to find her, on my own, some of those miserable fifty-franc bills bearing the likeness of Jean Racine. But nothing softened the coldness and hostility she had always shown me. I was never able to confide in her or ask her for help of any kind. Sometimes, like a mutt with no pedigree that has too often been left on its own, I feel the childish urge to set down in black and white just what she put me through, with her insensitivity and heartlessness. I keep it to myself. And I forgive her. It's all so distant now . . . I remember copying out these words by Léon Bloy at school: "Man has places in his heart which do not yet exist, and into them enters suffering, in order that they may have existence." But in this case it was suffering for nothing, the kind from which you can't even fashion a poem.

Our poverty should have brought us closer. One year—1963—they had to "reconnect" the gas mains in the apartment. Work needed to be done, and my mother didn't have the money to pay for it. Neither did I. We cooked our meals on an alcohol burner. We never put on the heat in the winter. That lack of money would haunt us for a long time. One afternoon in January 1970, we were so hard up that she dragged me to the pawnbroker's on Rue Pierre-Charron, where I hocked a fountain pen "made of gold with a diamond nib" that Maurice Chevalier had presented to me at a literary awards ceremony. They gave me only two hundred francs for it, which my mother pocketed, steely-eyed.

During all those years, we dreaded due dates. Rents on those old apartments, dilapidated since before the war, weren't very high at first. Then they started rising around 1966 as the neighborhood changed, along with its shops and residents. Please don't hold such details against me: they caused me some anxiety at the time. But it soon evaporated, as I believed in miracles and would lose myself in Balzacian dreams of wealth.

After those dismal meetings with my father, we never entered the building together. He would go in first, and I, per his instructions, would have to cool my heels for a while, pacing around the block. He concealed our meetings from the ersatz Mylène Demongeot. Usually I saw him alone. One time, we had lunch with the marquis Philippe de D. and the meal was split between two restaurants, one on the Quai du Louvre and the other on the Quai des Grands-Augustins. My father told me that Philippe de D. was in the habit of lunching at several restaurants at a time, where he kept appointments with different people . . . He ordered his appetizer in one, his main course in another, and changed restaurants yet again for dessert.

The day when we followed Philippe
de D. from the Quai du Louvre to the Quai des
Grands-Augustins, he was wearing a kind of
military tunic. He claimed to have been a member of the Normandie-Niémen escadrille during
the war. My father often spent the weekend at
D.'s chateau in the Loire-Atlantique. He even
went on duckshoots there, which wasn't exactly
his style. I remember the few days in 1959 that
we spent in Sologne, at the home of Paul Bertholle, his wife, and the comte de Nalèche,
where I'd been afraid my father would abandon
me and those killers would drag me into their
blood sport. Just as he'd been "in business" with
Paul Bertholle, he was now "in business" with
Philippe de D. According to my father, D., in his
youth, had been a juvenile delinquent and had
even spent time in jail. He later showed me a
photo clipped from a back issue of *Détective* that
pictured D. in handcuffs. But D. had recently
come into a large inheritance from his grandmother (née de W.) and I imagine my father
needed him as an investor. Since the end of the

1950s, he had been pursuing a dream: to buy up shares in a business concern in Colombia. And he was surely counting on Philippe de D. to help him achieve his goal.

D. would marry a female racing driver and end his days ruined: as manager of a nightclub in Hammamet, then as garage owner in Bordeaux. For his part, my father would stay true to his Colombian dream for a few more years. In 1976, a friend sent me a document bearing this information: "Compagnie Financière Mocupia. Head office: 22 Rue Bergère, Paris 9. Tel. 770-76-94. French corporation. Board of Directors: President: Albert Rodolphe Modiano. Board: Charles Ruschewey, Léon-Michel Tesson . . . Kaffir Trust (Raoul Melenotte)."

I was able to identify the members of this board of directors—starting with Tesson, in September 1972, when a telegram from Tangier was mistakenly delivered to me instead of my father: 1194 TANGIER 34601 URGENT SETTLE RENT BERGERE—STOP—MY SECRETARY LAID UP—STOP. REPLY URGENT TESSON. This Tesson

was a financier in Tangier. As for Melenotte of
the Kaffir Trust, he had been a member of the
multinational administration of free zones.

In the years 1963 and 1964, I also met a
third man from the board of directors, Charles
Ruschewey. My father, hoping to dissuade me
from pursuing an overly "liberal" education,
pointed as an example of failure to this Charles
Ruschewey, who had been in the prestigious
khâgne program at Louis-le-Grand with Roger
Vailland and Robert Brasillach, and who had
never amounted to anything. Physically, he was
like a clergyman in civvies, a dirty-minded,
beer-swilling Swiss with steel-rimmed glasses
and fleshy lips, the type who'd secretly frequent
the "slags" of Geneva. In his fifties and divorced,
he was living with a plump, shorthaired woman
younger than he, in a windowless ground-floor
room in the 16th arrondissement. He must have
served as my father's factotum and "sidekick."
He looked like someone who would compromise
his principles at the drop of a hat, which didn't
stop him from lecturing me with a pedantry

worthy of Tartuffe. In 1976, I would run into
him on the stairs at Quai de Conti, aged and
puffy-faced and looking like a derelict, shopping
bag dangling from a sleepwalker's arm. And I
noticed he was living in the fourth-floor apartment that my father had recently abandoned for
Switzerland, though it contained not a stick of
furniture and the heat, water, and electricity had
all been cut off. He was squatting there with his
wife. She sent him out to do the shopping—no
doubt a few cans of food. She had become a real
harpy: I could hear her screeching every time
the poor man walked in the door. I don't imagine he was living off his director's fees from the
Compagnie Mocupia anymore. In 1976, again
in error, I received a report from that finance
company, according to which "our corporate
lawyer in Bogotá was instructed to file a claim
for compensation in the Colombian courts. For
reference, we inform you that Albert Modiano,
the president of your board of directors, is a director of the South American Timber Company

and represents our firm in this subsidiary." But life is cruel and unfair, and it shatters the fondest dreams: the president of the board of directors would never receive any compensation from Bogotá.

Christmas 1962. I don't remember whether there really was any snow that Christmas. In any case, in my mind I see it falling at night in heavy flakes on the road and the stables. I was met at the stud farm in Saint-Lô by Josée and Henri B.—Josée, the girl who used to look after me from ages eleven to fourteen, in my mother's absence. Henri, her husband, was the farm veterinarian. They were my last resort.

Over the following years, I'd often return to their place in Saint-Lô. The city they called "capital of the ruins" had been flattened by bombardments during the Normandy invasion, and many survivors had lost all trace or proof of their identity. They were still rebuilding Saint-Lô into the 1950s. Near the stud farm, there was a zone of temporary workers' huts. I would go to

the Café du Balcon and the town library; sometimes Henri would take me to the neighboring
farms, where he treated animals on call, even at
night. And at night, thinking of all those horses
standing guard around me or sleeping in their
stalls, I was relieved that they, at least, would
not be taken to the slaughterhouse, like the line
of horses I had seen one morning at the Porte
Brancion.

I made a few girlfriends in Saint-Lô. One
lived at the power plant. Another, at eighteen,
wanted to go to Paris and enroll in the Conser-
vatory. She told me of her plans in a café near
the train station. In the provinces, in Annecy, in
Saint-Lô, it was still a time when every dream
and nighttime stroll ended up at the station,
where the train left for Paris.

I read Balzac's *Lost Illusions* that Christmas of
1962. I was still living in the same room on the
top floor of the house. Its window looked out
onto the main road. I remember that every Sunday, at midnight, an Algerian walked up that
road toward the workers' huts, talking softly

to himself. And this evening, forty years later, Saint-Lô reminds me of the lit window in *The Crimson Curtain*—as if I'd forgotten to turn off the light in my old room or in my youth. Barbey d'Aurevilly was born around there. I had once visited his former house.

Nineteen sixty-three. Nineteen sixty-four. The years blend together. Days of indolence, days of rain . . . Still, I sometimes entered a trancelike state in which I escaped the drabness, a mixture of giddiness and lethargy, like when you walk the streets in springtime after being up all night.

Nineteen sixty-four. I met a girl named Catherine in a café on Boulevard de la Gare, and she had the same grace and Parisian accent as Arletty. I remember the spring that year. The leaves on the chestnut trees along the elevated metro. Boulevard de la Gare, its squat houses not yet demolished.

My mother got a bit part in a play by François Billetdoux at the Théâtre de l'Ambigu: *Comment va le monde, môssieu? Il tourne, môssieu . . .* Boris Vian's widow, Ursula Kübler, was also in the cast. She drove a red Morgan. Sometimes I went to visit her and her friend Hot d'Déé in Cité Véron. She showed me how she used to do the "bear dance" with Boris Vian. It moved me to see the complete set of Boris Vian's records.

In July, I took refuge in Saint-Lô. Idle afternoons. I frequented the town library and met a blonde. She was spending her holidays in a villa in the hills of Trouville, with her kids and dogs. During the Occupation, when she was fourteen, she had lived at the Legion of Honor school in Saint-Denis. A "schoolgirl of old boarding-schools." My mother wrote me: "If you're happy there, it would be best if you stayed as long as possible. I'm living on practically nothing, and this way I can send the rest of the money I owe Galeries Lafayette."

In September, in Saint-Lô, another letter from my mother: "I don't think we'll have any heating this winter, but we'll manage. So I need you, my son, to send me all the money you have left." At the time, I made a modest living by "brokering" used books. And in still another letter, a hopeful note: "The coming winter surely won't be as harsh as the one we've been through . . ."

I received a phone call from my father. He

had enrolled me, without asking, in advanced literature courses at the Lycée Michel-Montaigne in Bordeaux. He was, he said, "in charge of my schooling." He made an appointment with me for the following day, at the cafeteria of the railway station in Caen. We took the first train for Paris. At Saint-Lazare, the ersatz Mylène Demongeot was waiting for us and drove us to the Gare d'Austerlitz. I realized that she was the one who had insisted on my exile, far from Paris. My father asked me to give the ersatz Mylène Demongeot, as a token of reconciliation, an amethyst ring I was wearing, a parting gift from my friend, the "schoolgirl of old boarding schools." I refused.

At the Gare d'Austerlitz, my father and I caught the train to Bordeaux. I had no luggage, as if I were being kidnapped. I'd agreed to leave with him in hopes of talking things over between us: it was the first time in two years we'd been alone together, other than those furtive meetings in cafés.

We arrived in Bordeaux that evening. My

father took a room for the two of us at the Hôtel Splendide. The following days, we went to the shops on Rue Sainte-Catherine to buy my necessities for the school year—of which the Lycée Michel-Montaigne had sent my father a list. I tried to convince him that all this was pointless, but he stuck to his guns.

One evening, in front of the Grand Théâtre, I started running to try to lose him. And then I felt sorry for him. Again I tried to talk things over. Why was he always so eager to get rid of me? Wouldn't it be simpler if I just stayed in Paris? I was too old to be shut up in boarding schools . . . He didn't want to hear it. So then I pretended to give in. As before, we went to the movies . . . The Sunday evening before school began, he brought me to the Lycée Michel-Montaigne in a taxi. He gave me 150 francs and made me sign a receipt. Why? He waited in the taxi until I had disappeared through the front door of the school. I went up to the dormitory with my suitcase. The boarders treated me as a "new kid" and forced me to read aloud a text in

Greek. So I decided to run away. I left the school with my suitcase and went to have dinner at the restaurant Dubern, on Allée de Tourny, where my father had taken me on the previous days. Then I took a cab to the Gare Saint-Jean. And a night train to Paris. There was nothing left of the 150 francs. I was sorry not to have seen more of Bordeaux, the city of *The Unknown Sea;* not to have breathed in the scent of pines and their resin. The next day, in Paris, I ran into my father on the stairs in our building. He was stunned to see me. We would not speak to each other for a long time after that.

And the days and months passed. And the seasons. Sometimes I'd like to go back in time and relive those years better than I lived them then. But how?

I now took Rue Championnet at the hour of the afternoon when the sun is in your eyes. I spent my days in Montmartre in a kind of waking dream. I felt better there than anywhere else. The metro stop Lamarck-Caulaincourt, with its rising elevator and the San Cristobal midway up the steps. The café at the Terrass Hôtel. For brief moments, I was happy. Get-togethers at 7 P.M. at the Rêve. The icy handrail on Rue Berthe. And me, always short of breath.

On Thursday, April 8, 1965, judging from an old diary, my mother and I didn't have a cent. She forced me to go ring at my father's door and demand some money. I climbed the stairs with a leaden heart. I'd intended not to ring, but my mother was glaring up at me from the landing, eyes and chin tragic, foaming at the mouth. I rang. He slammed the door in my face. I rang again. The ersatz Mylène Demongeot screamed that she was going to call the police. I went back down to the third floor. The police came for me. My father was with them. They made both of us climb into the Black Maria parked in front of the building, under the dumbfounded eyes of the concierge. We sat on the bench, side by side. He didn't say a word to me. This was the first time in my life I found myself in a police van, and as it happened, it was with my father. He had already been through this before, in February

1942 and in the winter of 1943, when he'd been picked up by the French inspectors of the Jewish Affairs police.

The Black Maria followed Rue des Saints-Pères, then Boulevard Saint-Germain. It stopped at a red light in front of the Deux Magots. We arrived at the police station on Rue de l'Abbaye. My father pressed charges with the superintendent. He called me a "hooligan" and said I'd come up to his place to "make trouble." The superintendent declared that the "next time" he'd keep me there. I could tell my father would have been perfectly content to leave me at that police station once and for all. We returned together to the Quai de Conti. I asked why he'd let the ersatz Mylène Demongeot call the police and why he'd pressed charges. He said nothing.

That same year, 1965—or perhaps 1964— my father demolished the inner staircase connecting the two floors, and the apartments were separated for good. When I opened the door and stood in the small room filled with rubble, I found some of our childhood books, along with postcards addressed to my brother that had remained on the fourth floor, there among the debris, torn in pieces. May and June. Still in Montmartre. It was nice out. I was at a café on Rue des Abbesses, in the springtime.

July. Night train, standing in the corridor. Vienna. I spend a few nights in a seedy hotel near the Westbahnhof. Then I hole up in a room behind the Karlskirche. I meet all sorts of people at the Café Hawelka. One evening, I celebrate my twentieth birthday with them.

We sunbathed in the gardens of Potzleinsdorf, and also in a little shack in a working-class allotment near Heiligenstadt. The Café Rabe, a gloomy beer hall near the Graben, was always empty and you could listen to songs by Piaf. And still that slight giddiness mixed with lethargy, in the summer streets, as if after a sleepless night.

Sometimes we went up to the Czech and Hungarian borders. A large field. Watchtowers. If you walked in the field, they would fire at you.

I left Vienna at the beginning of September. *Sag' beim Abschied leise "Servus,"* as the song goes.

A passage by our Joseph Roth calls to mind the city I haven't seen in forty years. Will I ever see it again? "You had to grab these shy, fleeting evenings before they disappeared, and what I liked best was to catch them in the parks, the Volksgarten or the Prater, and then to savor the last sweetest lingering of them in a café, where they seeped in, gentle and mild, like a fragrance . . ."

Night train in second class, at the Westbahnhof, Vienna to Geneva. I arrived in Geneva at the end of the afternoon. I caught the bus for Annecy. In Annecy, night had fallen. It was pouring. I was broke. I went into the Hôtel d'Angleterre on Rue Royale, with no idea how I'd pay for a room. I no longer recognized Annecy, which that evening was a ghost town in the rain. They had demolished the old hotel and derelict buildings near the station. The next day, I ran across some friends. Many had already left for military service. That evening, I thought I saw them pass by in the rain in uniform. As it turned out, I had fifty francs left. But the Hôtel d'Angleterre was expensive. During those few days, I had gone to the Collège Saint-Joseph in Thônes to visit my old literature teacher, Father Accambray. I had written him from Vienna, asking whether they might hire me as a proctor or assistant teacher for the coming year. I think I was trying to avoid Paris and my poor parents, who had given me no moral support whatsoever and had left me with my back to the wall. I've found two letters from Father Accambray: "I'd love it if the school year could start with you as a teacher in our house. I've spoken with the Superior. The teaching staff is full, but there could possibly be some movement before the end of August, which I hope will happen so that you can join us." In the second, dated September 7, 1965, he writes: "The teaching schedule on which I've been working these past few days clearly shows, alas, that we have more than enough staff for the 1965–66 school year. We simply can't offer you any work, even part-time . . ."

But life continued with no clear sense of why at a given moment you found yourself with certain individuals rather than others, in certain places rather than others, and whether the film was in the original language or dubbed. These days, all that remain in my memory are brief sequences. I enrolled in the Faculty of Literature to prolong my military deferment. I never went to classes and was a phantom student. Jean Normand (alias Jean Duval) came to live at Quai de Conti for several months, in the small room that had once contained the inner staircase connecting the third and fourth floors. He worked in a real estate office but was persona non grata in Paris. That's something I would learn later. My mother had met him around 1955. Normand was twenty-seven then and had just served time in prison for burglary. As it happened, he had committed some of those burglaries, while still very young, with Suzanne Bouquerau, the woman my brother and I lived with in Jouy-en-Josas. He must have gone back to jail since then, as he was in Poissy prison in 1959. He made some basic restorations to the dilapidated room and I'm sure he gave my mother money. I was very fond of this Normand (alias Duval). One evening, he quietly left a hundred-franc bill on the mantelpiece of my room, which I discovered only after he'd gone. He drove a Jaguar, and the following year, at the time of the Ben Barka Affair, I read in the papers that they'd nicknamed him "the tall man with the Jaguar."

An incident, from 1965 or '66: It's ten o'clock at night and I'm alone in the apartment. I hear heavy footsteps upstairs, at my father's, and the crash of furniture being knocked over and windows being smashed. Then silence. I open the door to the landing. Coming from the fourth floor, two stocky fellows who look like thugs or plainclothes cops hurtle down the stairs. I ask them what's going on. One of them makes an authoritarian gesture and tells me sharply to "go back inside." I hear footfalls in my father's apartment. So he was there . . . I'm tempted to phone him, but we haven't seen each other since our trip to Bordeaux, and I'm certain he'll hang up. Two years later, I ask him what happened that night. He claims not to know what I'm talking about. I believe that man could have worn down ten examining magistrates.

That autumn of 1965, on evenings when I had a few five-franc bills bearing the likeness of Victor Hugo, I patronized a restaurant near the Lutèce theater. And I hid out in a room on Avenue Félix-Faure in the 15th arrondissement, where a friend was storing a ten-year collection of *Paris-Turf:* he used them to make arcane statistical calculations for his bets at Auteuil and Longchamp. Pie in the sky. And yet I remember finding my bearings in that Grenelle neighborhood, thanks to those razor-straight backstreets that flowed down to the Seine. Sometimes I'd take a taxi very late at night. The ride cost five francs. At the edge of the 15th arrondissement, the police often checked for minors. I had altered the birthdate on my passport to give myself legal age, transforming 1945 into 1943.

Raymond Queneau was kind enough to receive me on Saturdays. Often, at the beginning of the afternoon, we'd return from Neuilly along

the Left Bank. He told me of a walk he had taken
with Boris Vian to a dead-end street that almost
no one knew, at the far end of the 13th arrondissement, between the Quai de la Gare and the
Austerlitz train tracks: Rue de la Croix-Jarry.
He recommended I go there. I've read that the
times Queneau was happiest were when he wan-
dered around in the afternoon, thinking up his
articles about Paris for *L'Intransigeant*. I wonder
whether those dead years that I'm invoking here
are worth it. Like Queneau, I was really myself
only when I could be alone in the streets, seeking out curiosities like the Asnières dog cemetery. I had two dogs at the time. Their names
were Jacques and Paul. In Jouy-en-Josas, in 1952,
my brother and I had a dog called Peggy, who
got run over one afternoon on Rue du Docteur-
Kurzenne. Queneau was very fond of dogs.

   He told me of a western that depicted a fierce
battle between the Indians and the Basques. The
presence of Basques had struck him as very odd
and very funny. I finally tracked down the film:
it's called *Thunder in the Sun*. The synopsis indeed

says that it's about Indians versus Basques. I'd like to see this film in memory of Queneau, in a revival house they've forgotten to tear down, in some obscure corner of the city. Queneau's laugh. Part geyser, part rattle. But I have no talent for metaphor. It was simply Queneau's laugh.

Nineteen sixty-six. One evening in January, Quai de Conti. Jean Normand comes home around eleven o'clock. I'm alone with him in the apartment. The radio is on. They announce the suicide of Georges Figon in a studio on Rue des Renaudes, just as the police were breaking down the door. He was a protagonist in the Ben Barka Affair. Normand turns pale and makes a phone call, reads someone the riot act, quickly hangs up. He explains that he and Figon had had dinner together not an hour before and that Figon was an old friend, since their school days at the Collège Sainte-Barbe. He doesn't tell me that they had served time together in Poissy, as I found out later.

And minor events slip by, slide off you without

leaving much trace. You feel as if you can't yet live your real life, as if you're a stowaway. Of that fraudulent existence, I still recall a few scraps. At Easter, I came across a magazine article concerning Jean Normand and Ben Barka's murder. The article was headlined: "Why haven't they questioned this man?" A large photo of Normand, with the caption: "He has hatchet features that look like they were cut with a jackhammer. His name is Normand, but he goes by Duval. Figon called him 'the tall man with the Jag.' Normand, or Duval, had known Georges Figon for years . . ."

That spring, I sometimes stayed at the home of Marjane L. on Rue du Regard. Her apartment was the meeting place for a gang of individuals who circulated aimlessly among Saint-Germain-des-Prés, Montparnasse, and Belgium. Some, who had already discovered psychedelia, used it as a stopover between trips to Ibiza. But one might also run into a certain Pierre Duvelz (or Duveltz): blond, mid-thirties, mustache, and glen plaid suits. He spoke French with a distinguished, international accent, displayed military decorations on his lapel, and claimed to have been in officer candidate school at Saint-Maixent and married to a "Guinness heiress." He placed phone calls to embassies. He was often with a moronic-looking nonentity who doted on him, and he boasted of his love affair with an Iranian woman.

Other shadows, among them a certain Gérard Marciano. And so many more besides, whom I've forgotten and who must have died since then, violently.

That spring of 1966 in Paris, I felt a change in the atmosphere, a variation in climate that I had already sensed in 1958, at age thirteen, and again at the end of the Algerian War. But this time, there was no major event occurring in France, no tipping point—or else I've forgotten. Moreover, to my shame, I couldn't tell you what was happening in the world in April 1966. We were emerging from a tunnel, but as for what tunnel it was, I haven't a clue. And that breath of fresh air was something we hadn't experienced in previous seasons. Was it merely the illusion of twenty-year-olds who always think the world began with them? The air felt lighter to me that spring.

Following the Ben Barka Affair, Jean Normand stopped living at Quai de Conti and vanished mysteriously. Around May or June, I was summoned by the vice squad and told to report to an Inspector Langlais. He questioned me for three solid hours in one of their offices, amid cops coming and going, and typed up my answers. To my amazement, he told me that someone had accused me of being a drug user and dealer, and he showed me a mug shot of Gérard Marciano, whom I'd met once or twice on Rue du Regard. My name was apparently in his address book. I said I didn't know him. The inspector made me show him my arms to check for needle tracks. He threatened to search Quai de Conti and Avenue Félix-Faure, but apparently he didn't know about Rue du Regard—which surprised me, since the abovementioned Gérard Marciano used to frequent that apartment. He let me go, warning that I might have to come back for more questions. Sadly, they never ask you the right ones.

I alerted Marjane L. about the vice squad and Gérard Marciano, who never showed his face again. Pierre Duvelz, for his part, got himself arrested a few days later in a gun shop, while trying to buy or sell a revolver. Duvelz was a crook, with an arrest warrant out for him. And I committed a bad deed: I stole Duvelz's wardrobe, which had remained behind at Marjane L.'s and contained some very elegant suits, and I swiped an antique music box belonging to the owners of the apartment Marjane L. was renting. I found a secondhand goods dealer on Rue des Jardins-Saint-Paul and sold him the lot for five hundred francs. He told me he came from a family of scrap merchants in Clichy and that he'd been tight with Joseph Joinovici. If I had any other items to get rid of, just call. He gave me an extra hundred francs, evidently moved by my shyness. The following year, I would make restitution for that bad deed. I used my first author's royalties to repay the theft of the music box. I would gladly have bought Duvelz a few suits, but I never heard from him again.

Let's be honest to the bitter end: In 1963, my mother and I had sold to a Pole we knew, who worked at the flea market, the four practically new suits, along with shirts and three pairs of shoes with pale wood shoe trees, that my father's friend Robert Fly had left in a closet. He, too, like Duvelz, favored glen plaid suits and had disappeared overnight. We were flat broke that afternoon. Just barely the few coins the grocer on Rue Dauphine had given me for the bottle deposit. At the time, a baguette cost forty-four centimes. After that, I stole books from private individuals or libraries. I sold them because I needed the money. A first printing of *Swann's Way*, published by Grasset; a first edition of Artaud inscribed to Malraux; signed novels by Montherlant, letters from Céline, a "table of the royal military houses" published in 1819, a clandestine edition of Verlaine's *Femmes* and *Hombres*, dozens of Pléiade volumes and art books . . . From the moment I started writing, I never again committed another theft. Now and then, my mother, though she never stopped putting on airs, might also filch a few "luxury" items and leather goods from the shelves of the Belle Jardinière or other department stores. She was never caught in the act.

But time is growing short, the summer of 1966 is upon us, and with it what they called being "of age." I took refuge in the neighborhood around Boulevard Kellermann, and I hung out at the nearby Cité Universitaire, with its large lawns, restaurants, cafeteria, cinema, and resident students. I made friends with Moroccans, Algerians, Yugoslavians, Cubans, Egyptians, Turks . . .

In June, my father and I reconciled. I went to meet him many times in the lobby of the Hôtel Lutétia. But I realized he did not have my best interests at heart. He tried to persuade me to enlist before my draft number came up. He would see to it himself, he said, that I was stationed in the Reuilly barracks. I pretended to acquiesce so that I could get some money out of him, just enough to spend my last holidays as a "civvy": you can't turn down a future soldier. He was convinced I'd soon be in uniform. I would turn twenty-one and he'd finally be rid of me. He doled out three hundred francs, the only "pocket" money he ever gave me. I was so delighted with this "bonus" that I would gladly have promised to join the Foreign Legion. And I thought of his mysterious compulsion always to push me away: schools, Bordeaux, the police station, the army . . .

Leave as soon as possible, before autumn and the barracks. July 1, early morning, Gare de Lyon. Second-class train car, packed. The holidays had just begun. I spent most of the trip standing in the corridor. Nearly ten hours to reach the Midi. The train skirted the seashore. Les Issambres. Sainte-Maxime. Fleeting impression of freedom and adventure. Among the reference points of my life, summers will always matter, even though they ultimately all blend together because of their eternal noon.

I rented a room overlooking the small main

square of La Garde-Freinet. It was there, at an outdoor table of a café-restaurant one afternoon, in the shade, that I started writing my first novel. The post office across the square was open only two hours a day, in this village of sunlight and somnolence. One evening that summer, I turned twenty-one, and the next day I was supposed to take the return train.

Back in Paris, I kept out of sight. August. In the evenings, I went to the Fontainebleau cinema on Avenue d'Italie, or to the restaurant La Cascade on Avenue Reille . . . I gave my father a phone number, Gobelins 71-91. He called at nine in the morning. I let the alarm ring and slept until two in the afternoon. I continued working on my novel. I saw my father one last time, in a café on the corner of Rue de Babylone and Boulevard Raspail. Then there was this exchange of letters between us: "ALBERT RODOLPHE MODIANO 15 QUAI DE CONTI Paris VI, August 3, 1966. Dear Patrick, In case you decide to act according to your whims and disregard my decisions, the situation will be as follows: You are twenty-one years old; you are therefore an adult and I am no longer responsible for you. Consequently, you may no longer count on me for any assistance or support of any kind, whether material or moral. My decision regarding you is simple and nonnegotiable, and you can accept it or not: you terminate your deferment before August 10 in order to enlist in November. On Wednesday morning, we had agreed to go to the Reuilly Barracks to terminate your deferment. We were supposed to meet at 12:30; I waited for you until 1:15 and, true to your usual practice as a dishonest and ill-bred youngster, you neither showed up for our meeting nor even took the trouble to call with an apology. I can tell you that this is the last time you'll have the opportunity to show me such cowardice. You therefore have a choice: you can have your own way, entirely and definitively renouncing my support, or you can comply with my decision. It's up to you. Whichever you choose, I can state categorically that life will teach you once again that your father was right. Albert MODIANO. PS—I will add that I expressly convened the members of my family, whom I informed of the situation and who completely agree with me." What family? One he had rented for the occasion?

"Paris, August 4, 1966. Dear Sir: You are aware that in the last century, the 'recruiting sergeants' used to get their victims drunk before enlisting them. The haste with which you tried to drag me to the Reuilly barracks reminded me of that system. Military service offers you a splendid opportunity to be rid of me. The 'moral support' you promised me last week will now be taken over by the corporals. As for 'material support,' it will be redundant, as I will have room and board at the barracks. In short, I have decided to act according to my whims and disregard your decisions. My situation will therefore be as follows: I am twenty-one years old, I am an adult, you are no longer responsible for me. Consequently, I will no longer count on you for any assistance or support of any kind, whether material or moral."

Today, I regret writing him that letter. But

what was I to do? I didn't hold it against him; moreover, I've never held anything against him. I was merely afraid of finding myself prisoner in some barracks in the East. If he'd known me ten years later—as Mireille Ourousov had said—there wouldn't have been the slightest problem between us. He would have enjoyed talking literature with me, and I could have asked him about his financial dealings and mysterious past. And so, in another life, we walk arm in arm, not hiding our meetings from anyone.

"ALBERT RODOLPHE MODIANO 15 QUAI DE CONTI Paris VI, August 9, 1966. I've received your letter of August 4th, addressed not to your father but to 'Dear Sir,' in whom I must recognize myself. Your bad faith and hypocrisy have gone too far. It's the Bordeaux business all over again. My decision regarding your enlistment in the military in November was not made lightly. I considered it indispensable not only that you get a change of scenery, but also that you conduct your life by discipline rather than whimsy.

Your insolence is contemptible. Your decision has been duly noted. ALBERT MODIANO." I never saw him again.

Autumn in Paris. I continue working on my novel, in the evenings, in a room in one of the huge apartment buildings on Boulevard Kellermann and in the two cafés at the end of Rue de l'Amiral-Mouchez.

One evening, and I wonder why, I found myself with some people on the other bank of the Seine, at the home of Georges and Kiki Daragane, the woman for whom I'd run away from school at age fourteen and a half. She had been living in Brussels at the time and my mother would have her over at Quai de Conti. Since then, some science-fiction writers from Saint-Germain-des-Prés and a few artists from the Panic Movement had been buzzing around her. They must have been courting her, and she granting them her favors, under the placid eye of her husband. Georges Daragane was a Brussels industrialist and a pillar of the Café du Flore, where he remained ensconced on a bench from nine until midnight, no doubt recapturing the youth he'd lost in Belgium . . . Kiki and I talked about the past and the already distant time of my adolescence, when, she told me, my father would take me in the evening to the restaurant Charlot, "the seafood king" . . . She retained a fond memory of my father. He'd been a charmer, before taking up with the ersatz Mylène Demongeot. Nathalie, the airline stewardess he'd met in 1950 on the Paris-Brazzaville flight, later told me that when he was hard up, my father took her to dinner not at Charlot the seafood king but at Roger's Fries . . . I shyly asked Georges Daragane and Kiki to read my manuscript, as if I were not in their apartment but in the salon of Mme and M. de Caillavet.

Perhaps all those people, whom I met during the 1960s and never saw again, are still living in a kind of parallel world, impervious to time, with the same faces as back in those days. I was thinking of this a short while ago, on a deserted street, in the sun. "You are in Paris with the examining magistrate," as Apollinaire said in his poem. And the magistrate shows me photos, documents, evidence. And yet, my life—that wasn't exactly it.

The spring of 1967. The lawns of the Cité Universitaire. The Parc Montsouris. At noon, the workers from the SNECMA aviation plant gathered at the café on the ground floor of the building. Place des Peupliers, on the afternoon in June when I learned they'd accepted my first book. The SNECMA plant at night, like a huge cargo ship run aground on Boulevard Kellermann.

One June evening at the Théâtre de l'Atelier on Place Dancourt. A curious play by Audiberti: *Coeur à cuire*. Roger worked at the Atelier as stage manager. The evening of Roger and Chantal's wedding, I had dined with them in the small apartment of someone whose name I don't remember, on that same Place Dancourt where the light shimmers from the street lamps. Then they had driven away toward the outer suburbs.

That evening, I felt unburdened for the first time in my life. The threat that had weighed on me for so many years, kept me on edge, had dissolved in the Paris air. I had set sail before the worm-eaten wharf could collapse. It was time.

PATRICK MODIANO, winner of the 2014 Nobel Prize in Literature, was born in Boulogne-Billancourt, France, in 1945, and was educated in Annecy and Paris. He published his first novel, *La Place de l'Etoile*, in 1968. In 1978, he was awarded the Prix Goncourt for *Rue des Boutiques Obscures* (published in English as *Missing Person*), and in 1996 he received the Grand Prix National des Lettres for his body of work. Modiano's other writings include a book-length interview with the writer Emmanuel Berl and, with Louis Malle, the screenplay for *Lacombe Lucien*.

MARK POLIZZOTTI's books include the collaborative novel *S.* (1991), *Lautréamont Nomad* (1994), *Revolution of the Mind: The Life of André Breton* (Farrar, Straus and Giroux, 1995; rev. ed., 2009), *Luis Buñuel's Los Olvidados* (British Film Institute, 2006), and *Bob Dylan: Highway 61 Revisited* (Continuum, 2006). His articles and reviews have appeared in the *New Republic*, the *Wall Street Journal*, *ARTnews*, the *Nation*, *Parnassus*, *Partisan Review*, *Bookforum*, and elsewhere. The translator of more than forty books from the French, including works by Patrick Modiano, Gustave Flaubert, Marguerite Duras, André Breton, Raymond Roussel, and Jean Echenoz, he directs the publications program at The Metropolitan Museum of Art in New York.